D0629267

Motivation,
Emotions,
and
Leadership

The Structure of Human Motivation

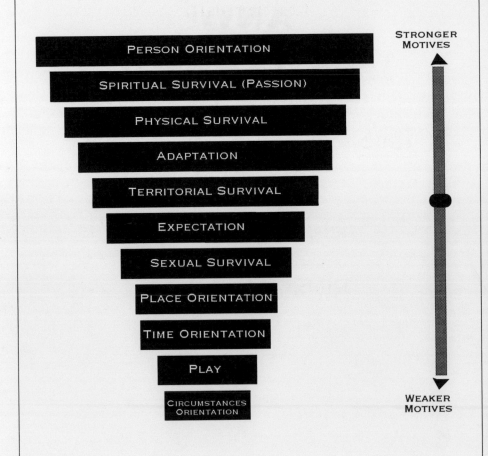

MOTIVATION, EMOTIONS, AND LEADERSHIP

The Silent Side of Management

Richard C. Maddock
and
Richard L. Fulton

QUORUM BOOKS
Westport, Connecticut • London

Library of Congress Cataloging-in-Publication Data

Maddock, Richard C.
  Motivation, emotions, and leadership : the silent side of
management / Richard C. Maddock, Richard L. Fulton.
      p.   cm.
  Includes bibliographical references and index.
  ISBN 1–56720–151–2 (alk. paper)
  1. Employee motivation. 2. Emotions. 3. Leadership. I. Fulton,
Richard L. II. Title.
  HF5549.5.M63M33   1998
  658.3'14—dc21   98–6021

British Library Cataloguing in Publication Data is available.

Library of Congress Catalog Card Number: 98–6021
ISBN: 1–56720–151–2

First published in 1998

Quorum Books, 88 Post Road West, Westport, CT 06881
An imprint of Greenwood Publishing Group, Inc.

Printed in the United States of America

The paper used in this book complies with the
Permanent Paper Standard issued by the National
Information Standards Organization (Z39.48–1984).

10 9 8 7 6 5 4 3 2 1

This book is dedicated
to our parents

In memory of
Richard C. Maddock, DDS
and
Isabel Maddock

In honor of
Jim Fulton
and
Phyllis Fulton

Contents

Acknowledgments

The authors wish to thank Becky Adair, Vickey Fulton and Taylor Maddock for their tireless work and devotion to the manuscript.

Special thanks are offered to Dr. Charles Long at the University of Memphis; Dr. David Cox at Arkansas State University in Jonesboro; and to Eric Valentine, Doug Goldenberg-Hart and Gillian von N. Beebe at Quorum Books.

As always, the authors are indebted to Dr. Paul Fleischman and Dr. Ray Sexton for their penetrating insight into the perplexing subject of human motivation.

Introduction

MANY OF OUR THEORIES OF LEADERSHIP NO LONGER APPLY

Much of what has been learned about leadership in the 1980s and '90s has had to be shelved.

Some religious leaders who were able to command and control large empires and collect untold millions in contributions via televised services turned out to be devoid of character. Similarly, as was seen in the presidential elections that brought Bill Clinton into office, character is really not a very important issue when it comes to choosing a leader. This observation was seconded by voters in Illinois who chose Dan Rostenkowski and Mel Reynolds, by stockholders of the Bendix Corporation who chose William Agee as CEO, and by the numerous people who felt that O. J. Simpson was a paragon of virtue because of his professional stature in sports and on television. Character appears to be neither a necessary nor a sufficient condition of leadership. Surprising, isn't it?

It was also determined that leadership was not gender related. In the 1980s and '90s, women replaced men in positions of leadership in record numbers, and the contribution made by women to organizations and groups, in management and in overall direction, was very impressive.

It was learned that leadership and the selection or identification of leaders was not within the exclusive purview or scope of any one group, such as managers, psychologists, educators or politicians. Although some in these groups may claim authenticity or authority in the field, it is an empty claim because no one group has provided the insight to enable us to readily and unmistakingly identify individuals who are, or will become, leaders.

It was also learned that successful leadership is not exclusively defined or differentiated by any one particular approach or school of psychology or management, such as those who promote democratic leadership, lassaiz-faire leadership, autocratic leadership, and so on.

And finally, after all the debates and arguments, there is still no answer to the question, "Are leaders born, or are they made?" Humankind has been to the moon and back several times, but we still don't know that much about leaders and leadership.

So what is leadership? What are the ingredients of being a leader? How does someone rise to the top of an organization, politics, sports, religion, entertainment or any other profession?

LEADERSHIP AS MOTIVATION AND MOTIVATION AS EMOTION

This book is about the substance of leadership, which can be defined in one word: *motivation*. Even though you previously may have heard that leadership is motivation, what you have not heard, if you stop to think about it, is what motivation is exactly. Motivation, surprisingly enough, has never been defined in a scientifically acceptable, reasonable and legitimate manner. It has not even been defined in a practical, commonsense or useful manner.

One reason that motivation has not been defined is because it is too close to emotion to allow it to be defined, and no one wants to flirt with emotion. This is particularly true in the workplace. Because motivation and emotion are twins, the tendency is to avoid both. If emotion is volatile, then motivation must be equally as volatile.

How do we avoid emotion in the workplace, the courtroom, church or in a civic organization? First, we do it in the way in which we dress. Subdued, asexual, conservative and "tasteful" dress is always emphasized for both men and women. This is not even discussed. We take it for granted.

Second, we avoid emotion in the way in which we address other people. For example: An organization was in the process of isolating one of its managers. Isolation is the first step toward termination and eliminates the process of having to deal with a person head on or with all the emotions that accompany termination. When the manager flew more than 2,000 miles to attend a department heads' meeting, he was told by the corporation that he couldn't attend the meeting because "we don't have enough chairs." He had no choice but to go back home and start packing.

Third, we deal with emotion by using very carefully chosen, camouflaged words and phrases and by expressing ourselves nonverbally as much as possible. "Not having any chairs" is an example of a nonverbal expression. Instead of saying "I'm angry," we say "I'm concerned." Instead of saying "You're fired!" we isolate a person from the people and the routines that he or she has worked with for many years, until the individual becomes so uncomfortable that he or she resigns.

Finally, when we do deal with emotion, we do it artificially and superficially. We deal only with surface issues that will not cause embarrassment to the organization and will not yield information that management does not want to hear. When workers are angry, we conduct a "job satisfaction" survey. When changes are to be made, we bring in outside consultants to do the dirty work of announcing the bad news.

There are many other ways that we avoid emotion, particularly in the workplace. The result of all this avoidance is that going to work or going anyplace else where emotion is not tolerated becomes arduous and difficult. It becomes a struggle to hold these feelings in all day long, not to express them or show them in any way and to pretend they do not exist. Eventually, this struggle with the expression or nonexpression of emotion becomes intolerable, and as a result, productivity and output suffer.

Even psychologists and psychiatrists, who are in the business of "curing" mental illness, do it by telling patients to ignore and isolate emotions and feelings. Psychiatrists have pills for it. The most common pills are the benzodiazepines: Valium, Librium and Xanax. What they often do not tell patients is that these medications are highly addictive and may also defeat their more pleasant emotions, like sex. Psychologists do not prescribe pills, but help patients to "control" anger rather than deal with it directly. The word "control" means, in this context, "avoid."

To prepare future leaders to deal with motivation, this volume introduces them to emotion. For most, it will be their first introduction. It may cause some difficulty or discomfort, but it is the first step to dealing with motivation, and only one step removed from the issue of leadership. This is because leadership is motivation, and leaders are, first and foremost, motivators.

Now an obvious question about motivation and leadership is, "Hasn't it already been said, in one way or another, that motivation *is* leadership?" The answer is "Yes, it has been said." But the problem is that no one has ever defined motivation. Psychologists, to whom we would normally look for an adequate definition of leadership, have abdicated. They have done well discussing what motivates animals, but have been strangely silent about what motivates people.

The next question is simply, "How do you know that you can define motivation, because up to this point no one has?" The answer to this question comes from three different and seemingly unrelated directions.

A THREE-DIMENSIONAL APPROACH TO MOTIVATION AND EMOTION

Our clear-cut and all-inclusive definition of human motivation springs from scientific research that has been carried out since the 1970s, not only by us but also by others in three unrelated and seemingly disconnected areas.

First, our research since the 1970s has been with consumers, the products they use and the advertising that has been aimed at them. Research in this area has allowed us to find out what people really want, because we study them where they spend their money! From that point, it is only one more step to determining their motivation. A considerable portion of our work with consumers has been dedicated to advertising, and as is well known, advertising works! Many of the theories, approaches, explanations and methodologies in psychology, education, marketing and management do not work. But advertising does. Before advertisers are willing to spend $600,000 for a thirty-second spot during the Super Bowl, they have to be sure their advertising is effective and their message is motivational.

Second, the latter part of the 1980s and the early '90s were known as the Decade of the Brain. This nickname sprang from the fact that the U.S. government spent a considerable amount of money on brain research because it was the one organ about which the least was known. One area of particular interest was the limbic system, which is the center of the brain's emotional activity. Researchers and scientists working on government-funded projects have shared with us substantial information about emotion and motivation, including that they originate in the limbic system of the brain. This information has been enormously helpful in directing us in our quest to define motivation and all of its components or subcomponents. One of the subcomponents of motivation is leadership. Because of the work that has been carried out in neurological and neuroanatomical research, motivation can now be scientifically and accurately defined and described, which previously has not been the case.

The third dimension of support for our approach to human motivation is empirical validation, or statistics. This is a more traditional approach, whereas the first two are nontraditional. It is our feeling that all three are vital and necessary in order to arrive at a coherent, substantial and all-inclusive theory of human motivation. In the situations where we have defined and described human motives and motivations, we have carried out exploratory factor analyses in order to lend support to these motives and motivations. The results of these factor analyses are encouraging and are presented here in a nontechnical, explanatory manner.

MOTIVES, THE NONCONSCIOUS MIND AND SCIENCE

Motives, as we understand them, reside in what Freud described as the unconscious mind and in what we refer to as the *nonconscious*. Freud is responsible for the discovery and elaboration on the nonconscious and many of its components (Jones, 1955). However, many of Freud's explanations of motivation and motives are not consistent with natural selection and Darwin's discoveries about how the process of evolution works. Although Freud may have known about some of these discoveries, it is doubtful that he became intimately familiar or conversant with them. Therefore, although his contributions on the nonconscious and its existence are taken very seriously today, his theories on motivation are not.

The only other attempt to describe and define human motivation was by Maslow (1970). Maslow was a humanistic psychologist who defined human motivation in terms of a hierarchy or pyramid, with physiological needs being the most basic and "self-actualization" needs being the most complex. But Maslow never attempted to validate or substantiate his theory of motivation, statistically or in any other way. What is interesting, however, is that so many of today's managers, marketers, educators, psychologists and other professionals uncritically rely on Maslow's theory for an explanation of human motivation as the only explanation, when it is really not an explanation at all. Instead, it is an unvalidated belief system, more accurately compared with a religion than with science. Furthermore, Maslow's theory is not consistent with any recent scientific findings that we know of, and certainly not to Darwin's important discoveries. The failure of Maslow's approach in describing human motivation is discussed more fully in chapter 2.

The point here is that, although leadership has been defined as motivation in the past, motivation has never been defined. And even if you don't believe that leadership equals motivation, you still have to believe, by default, that motivation is part of the leadership picture. Bill Clinton, Jimmy Swaggart, Dan Rostenkowski and others may not have strong characters, but they certainly do know how to stand up in front of people and motivate them or move them toward action.

WHEN LEADERSHIP IS SEEN AS MOTIVATION

Defining leadership, in whole or in part, as motivation is not an attempt to oversimplify. It is instead an attempt to make our descriptions consistent with what we see in front of us. It is common sense. But there are also some secondary benefits. The reason that people have been running around in circles, asking questions like "Are leaders born?" "Are leaders made?" and "What is leadership?" is because so much of the leadership field has been tied to motivation, and motivation has not been defined. But as seen in this book, when it is defined, leadership will no longer be a circular, neverending debate or a can of worms. It will be operationally defined. Other benefits of being able to clearly define leadership include being able to train, select and identify leaders in organizations and to do the same with potential leaders. Programs that define leaders can be replicated, which is the goal of any scientific pursuit. Fewer flawed leaders will be chosen because our definition of leadership considers the nonconscious as well as the conscious components. These are the characteristics that people often try to hide when applying for a job or looking for a leadership position. This is often referred to as the *dark side*. We call it the *Silent Side*.

Finally, the tendency to avoid emotions, dark-side characteristics, affect and passion have resulted in theories of leadership and motivation that are basically bankrupt and insolvent. They describe, but they don't explain. They give a lot of details, but they don't give implications. In many ways, they itemize but they don't clarify.

Motivation is the Silent Side of leadership. It is wholistic because it looks at all facets of the person. It is selective because it only picks leaders who are capable of understanding motives and motivation, but it is inclusive because it will train and educate anyone who can understand. It broadens and widens the field of potential leaders. It offers performance above and beyond expectation. It amplifies and embellishes dedication, commitment and responsibility because it includes human emotion and passion rather than excluding these essential traits and ingredients.

REFERENCES

Fleischman, P. R. (1991). *The healing spirit. Explorations in religion and psychotherapy.* New York: Paragon.

Jones, E. (1955). *The life and work of Sigmund Freud* (Vol. 2). New York: Basic Books.

Maslow, A. H. (1970). *Motivation and personality* (2nd ed.). New York: Harper & Row.

Chapter 1

One More Time: What Is Leadership?

Rarely do you ever pick up a book or an article on leadership in which the question "What is leadership?" is not bantered back and forth with no firm resolve. In other words, you spend a couple of hours reading about what leadership is and what it isn't, and you still don't have any more of an idea than you did when you started. That's probably why there are so many different books about leadership. The debate continues.

That process is short-circuited in this volume. After a brief review of what leadership is and isn't, we get right into the problem and right at the definition. Like many things, it is simpler than it looks.

LEADERSHIP AS THE SUM TOTAL OF PERSONALITY TRAITS

An early review of leadership was carried out by Stogdill (1948), who reviewed research on personality and emergent leadership in a variety of unstructured groups. His conclusion was that measures of dominance, extroversion, sociability, ambition, responsibility, integrity, self-confidence, mood, emotional control, diplomacy and co-operativeness were positively related to emergent leadership. In a model endorsed by Stogdill in 1974, Hogan, Curphy and Hogan (1994) indicated that this same format fits into the "Big Five" model of personality structure presently endorsed by many psychologists and personality theorists. This model holds that personality can be described in terms of five broad dimensions: surgency, agreeableness, conscientiousness, emotional stability and intellect. This model, according to Hogan et al., provides a common vocabulary for interpreting the results of all personality research. But as is seen here, personality is not the basis for leadership, nor is it the reason a person is chosen as a leader. There are many successful leaders with "bad personalities."

A good deal of the literature on leadership has focused on traits. But the problem is, who defines the traits that comprise leadership, and leaders? According to Hogan et al., traits can be defined by team or individual performance, subordinates, self-ratings, or negative factors they referred to as *derailments* because they derail a person's career. Traits can also be defined by psychological tests, if we assume that personality and personality factors are important. In addition, traits also may be defined in terms of how leaders build teams (Hallam & Campbell, 1992), by a person's orientation to psychology (Lucia, 1997), in terms of the amount of control exercised (Helton, 1997), or by any number of other factors.

Helton (1997) presented a number of factors she said are essential for leadership in a "new age," including vision, ability to handle change, self-awareness, a clear set of values, openness and trustworthiness. However, any such listing of traits can always be called incomplete, and when any of these traits are labeled *essential* there can always be found an exception. The whole reason that psychologists have not been employed very often in the selection of leaders, a fact lamented by Hogan, et al. (1994), is because many people disagree with the traits that psychologists consider important. For example, in a book on Mary Parker Follett, who was a guru in management and leadership theory in the 1930s and '40s, it is shown that she took psychologists at that time to task because of their assumption that all leaders had to be masterful, aggressive and dominating. The point is that whenever a trait theory of leadership is proposed, it will often be quickly opposed because it is not all inclusive, or is perhaps too inclusive.

For Hogan et al., leadership is a constellation of traits, primarily related to personality and personality variables. They all question why personality is such an important ingredient of the overall leadership profile, and why it is that more psychologists are not involved in the selection of leaders on the front end. Hogan et al.'s reasoning is that psychologists have access to sophisticated tests and measures that other people do not have, and so they are ideally suited to choose leaders and theoretically to rule out flawed and potentially defective leadership. Our answer to that question is, once again, "Leadership is not a series of traits." It is not personality, and it is not popularity.

LEADERSHIP AS EMPATHY AND UNDERSTANDING

For Lucia (1997), leadership is empathy. It is knowing how to listen to people and hear them out. According to Lucia, "effective leaders hear what others have to say and empathize with their issues" (p. 25). We agree. But empathy is not only an important ingredient of leadership, it is an important ingredient of all interpersonal encounters.

LEADERSHIP AS INTEGRITY AND SUBSTANCE

For Barone (1995), Plummer (1995), Crouse (1994) and many others, leadership is integrity, honesty and substance. For this group, leaders are people who can stand close examination, scrutiny and inspection. But in a world where time moves faster than it ever has before, things change; and they change very quickly. There are many who would agree with Barone, Plummer and others about the importance of integrity, but there are many who disagree.

On June 21, 1996, *USA Today* conducted a readers' survey in order to get an idea about who would be elected president: Bob Dole or Bill Clinton. At the time, it looked like Clinton already had it in the bag, but the character issue was a real stumbling block. Could Clinton really be re-elected after the exposure of his character deficiencies that surfaced during the first term? These included Paula Jones, Jennifer Flowers, Whitewater and procurement by the Arkansas State Police. The purpose of the *USA Today* survey was just to determine the importance of character and the role it plays.

The first question readers were asked about character was who they thought was more trustworthy: "Who do you think is the most honest and trustworthy?" Thirty-six percent said Clinton, and 62 percent said Dole.

The second question about character was, "Who shares your values?" Fifty-three percent said Clinton, and 43 percent said Dole.

Then there was a series of questions about the investigations. One of these questions asked, "Based on what you have heard or read, do you think the following people did something wrong or illegal?" Sixty-one percent felt that Bill Clinton had done "something illegal or unethical," and only 31 percent felt that he did nothing wrong. At that time, Hillary Clinton was also in the spotlight. Seventy-five percent thought that Hillary had done something illegal or unethical, and only 25 percent felt that she had done nothing wrong. There were also some questions about the White House staffers and other people with whom Clinton associated, and in general the results were the same: no faith and very little confidence.

But then the surprising question: "If the election were to be held *today* and Clinton and Dole were the only ones running, who would you vote for?" Fifty-seven percent said Clinton, and 38 percent said Dole. Why does that not amaze us?

Prior to the 1996 presidential election, voters felt that character was an important and substantial issue. Over the years, many prominent politicians saw their careers abruptly end because of the character issue. Looking back, it would appear that the American people would not tolerate a dishonest, deceptive or conniving leader. Wilbur Mills, Dan Rostenkowski, Richard Nixon, Gary Hart, Mel Reynolds and many others either left their elected positions or dropped out of sight because of the character issue. But that was before. Before 1996, Americans were convinced their leaders had to have, at a minimum, a rock solid and impenetrable character.

But the 1996 election was not the first surprise. Many Americans were surprised to find out that O. J. Simpson, who had assumed a conspicuous leadership role in both the Black and White communities, beat his wife on a regular basis and treated her badly at times. What a surprise! But as we look back, was it really a surprise? What is it about O. J. Simpson or Clinton that made them leaders, anyway? Does a leader have to have an honorable character? Do the voters or the viewers really care? The character issue is usually never brought out by the voters, anyway. Instead it is typically brought out by the competition, usually in a last-ditch effort to destroy and demolish an adversary, and usually when nothing else works and the numbers are looking bad. So it should not be that big a surprise that the voters and the viewers are willing to accept character flaws in their leaders. Because leadership is not character.

If leadership is not character, then what is it?

LEADERSHIP AS CHARISMA

Some say that leadership is charisma.

Meyer, Ross, and MacLean (1996) summarized a number of studies showing that people who work under a charismatic boss or leader generate more ideas and report greater job satisfaction than those who have more structured and traditional leadership. He references Robert House, a professor of business at the University of Pennsylvania, who found what he called "value-based leaders" who were better able to motivate their subordinates by articulating a vision of an exciting, challenging future. This is important, and part of the goal of this book is to show that leaders who appeal to a visual, graphic or photographic image are more successful than leaders who do not.

Sellers (1996), in an article that attempts to dissect and analyze the whole issue of charisma, summed it up when he said that because charismatic leaders are capable of getting people to visualize, they possess a remarkable ability to distill complex ideas into very simple messages. This alone should make them successful leaders.

Bass (1985) and Bycio, Hackett and Allen (1995) found in Bass' Multifactor Leadership Questionnaire (MLQ) that there were three factors of transformational leadership, of which charismatic leadership was the strongest. *Charismatic leadership* is defined as the amount of faith, respect and inspiration generated by a leader. The second factor, individualized consideration, refers to the degree and amount of attention given to followers by the leader. The third factor, intellectual stimulation, refers to the extent to which the leader enables followers to rethink the way they do things. The second and third factors have very high (.90 and .91) intercorrelations with the first factor, charisma.

But the fact is, there are many leaders who do not have charisma. There are leaders who are pessimistic and cynical. As Sellers (1996) observed, there are professions and occupations, such as dentistry, engineering or accounting, where charisma and personal magnetism make very little difference. Although charisma appears to be an important and perhaps even vital part of leadership, which is discussed in more detail later, charisma is not leadership. Leadership is not charisma. In fact, charisma is neither a necessary nor a sufficient cause of leadership.

Having ruled out personality traits, empathy, understanding and charisma, what is leadership?

LEADERSHIP AS MOTIVATION

Leadership is motivation. A leader is a motivator. It is just that simple. This explains a lot and also provides answers to many of the questions we have about leadership.

It explains why an individual with a "poor" or "marginal" personality can become a leader. Or why someone who does not have charisma can become a leader. Or why, according to Hogan et al., it has been so difficult to measure leadership. It explains why the whole concept of leadership is so evasive and elusive. As it turns out, we have been measuring the wrong thing. Leadership *is* motivation.

You may be thinking right now that there is really nothing new about what we are saying, and if this is true, then this is just one more of the hundreds of books that will be published this year about leadership. Each one will say something a little different, but essentially they are still asking the same two questions. These questions—"What is leadership?" and "Are leaders born, or are they made?"—will be asked repeatedly, and there will be no substantive, binding answers. But our position is that we are saying something different, and something that is new: Leadership is motivation. Not that this has not been said before in many ways, but the difference here is that motivation is defined: what it is, what it is not, and how it works. It is defined practically, neurologically, scientifically, empirically and psychologically, so there is no doubt about what motivation really is.

Once you understand motivation, you understand leadership. And with regard to the question, "Are leaders born or made?" you also understand that leaders can be made, after they come to learn and understand what motivation is all about.

Leadership is motivation.

REFERENCES

Barone, M. (1995). Bill, meet Niccolo: Bill Clinton's approach to leadership is the opposite of Prince Niccolo Machiavelli's. *U.S. News and World Report 119*(11), 59.

Bass, B. M. (1985). *Leadership and performance beyond expectations.* New York: The Free Press.

Bycio, P., Hackett, R. D., & Allen, J. S. (1995). Further assessments of Bass's (1985) conceptualization of transactional and transformational leadership. *Journal of Applied Psychology 80*(4), 468–478.

Crouse, J. S. (1994). Leadership: working from the inside out. *Vital Speeches 60*(19), 597.

Hallam, G. L., & Campbell, D. P. (1992, May). *Selecting team members? Start with a theory of team effectiveness.* Paper presented at the seventh annual meeting of the Society of Industrial and Organizational Psychology, Montreal, Quebec, Canada.

Helton, S. (1997). Leadership for a new age. *Nation's Business 85*(5), 18.

Hogan, R., Curphy, G. J., & Hogan, J. (1994). What we know about leadership. *American Psychologist 49*(6), 493–504.

Laver, R. (1996, September 30). Building a better boss: Studies show that the personality of a chief executive officer can have a major impact on profits and productivity. *Maclean's 109*(40), 41.

Lucia, A. (1997). Leaders know how to listen. *HR Focus 74*(4), 25.

Plummer, L. C. (1995). In pursuit of honest leadership. *FBI Law Enforcement Bulletin 65*(4), 16.

Sellers, P. (1996). What exactly is charisma? *Fortune 133*(1), 68.

Stogdill, R. M. (1948). Personal factors associated with leadership: A survey of the literature. *Journal of Personality 25*, 35–71.

Chapter 2

What Motivation Is, and What It Isn't

Because the term *motivation* is so essential to the understanding and definition of leadership, it needs to be carefully defined and explained. But in order to understand what motivation is, we first must understand what it is not. The reason for this is easily understood when we make an analogy to the smoker, alcoholic or drug addict, who says, "I don't need this stuff. I can quit any time I want to." But the real test comes when the substance is taken away.

LEADERSHIP IS MOTIVATION: THE LEADER IS A MOTIVATOR

We're not talking about the kind of motivator who comes to town and stirs everyone up and then leaves. Most of those who attend this type of "motivator's" lectures are back in the doldrums again before the "motivator" even leaves town. That is not motivation. Real motivation lasts longer than twenty-four hours. Real motivation follows the guidelines set by nature, not the ones set by men. Real motivation is the key to effective leadership, and leadership is the key to effective motivation.

So what is motivation?

MOTIVATION: IT'S MASLOW, ISN'T IT?

Generally, whenever anyone thinks about motivation, Maslow's theory immediately comes to mind. Maslow (1970) was a clinical psychologist who wrote a book on motivation and is the most often quoted guru on the subject. Even scientific articles that are filled with data and spectacular findings eventually get around to quoting Maslow, as if his blessing is required in order to legitimize the findings.

Most executives' offices in the 1970s and '80s almost always contained a little model pyramid on the desk. This was Maslow's hierarchy of needs, or motives. Maslow's hierarchy of motives has been the gospel for business executives and managers for several decades, as well as for educators and teachers. Because it was placed in a pyramid, it automatically created a mnemonic device. But the problem is that Maslow was wrong. That's why, when one searches the literature, there are all kinds of definitions of leadership, some of which include motivation and some of which don't.

Watson (1996), in an article entitled "Motivation: That's Maslow, Isn't It?", made this point very clearly. It was not his intent to criticize Maslow or his hierarchy. In fact, he was not concerned with the content of Maslow's theory, but instead the process of educating students at the graduate level in management. Basically, what Watson found is that graduate-level education in management is like a word association test. The teacher says "motivation" and the students, in a knee-jerk response, say "Maslow." The teacher says "management," and the students say "Drucker." The teacher says "quality" and the students say "Tom Peters." And so it goes.

The point here is that when students were pressed to explain or give a scholarly critique of Maslow's theory, they could not do it. When pressed further, they were asked why, if they had no real feeling for whether the theory was accurate or inaccurate, they automatically associated Maslow's theory with motivation. Their response was:

> You know, when you are studying you like to find things that you will easily remember for the exam. If there is a simple little diagram, then that's really good. It helps you to remember the theory. The theories that don't have nice little pictures get forgotten. (Watson, p. 457)

We have had the same experience with students in undergraduate and graduate classes. They are looking for a simplistic, reductionist argument that puts Maslow's approach to motivation in a single, solitary position, even though it has no predictive or explanatory value. However, it is easy to remember.

According to Maslow, people have to reach a graduated set of needs, moving from the basic to the increasingly sophisticated as those needs are successively gratified. Physical survival is the first and foremost need, according to Maslow. Spiritual concerns—referred to as *self-actualization*—come afterward and are important only after basic needs are met. In other words, if you are hungry and cold, spiritual needs are the last things about which you want to think. What you do want to think about are physical needs, like getting three squares and a warm place to flop.

It is unfortunate that Maslow's hierarchy has had such a widespread reception because it does not really explain motivation. However, it is understandable when explained the way that Watson explained it: It is simple, and it is graphic. The category that Maslow called *self-actualization* is hard to define, borders on elitism and opens the door to elitism: "I'm self-actualized and you're not!" Furthermore, his bottom-line category of physical survival needs does not work either. Many people have known at least one person who, on the surface, seemed to have everything they ever wanted or needed, then got in their SL600, drove to the city dump, stuck a .357 in their mouth and blew out their brains. Suicide is the most common form of death among adolescents, second only to traffic accidents. It is also a leading cause of death among adults. Whatever it is that motivates someone to commit or even attempt suicide is not covered by Maslow's theory. And although this is not within the bounds of discussion in this book, nevertheless a theory that cannot explain one aspect of human behavior, such as suicide, will be grossly inadequate in terms of explaining other aspects, such as leadership. If a theory cannot explain all facets of human behavior, then it cannot explain any.

Watson also showed in his article that when graduate students are subjected to an intensive group analysis and assessment of Maslow's theory, it does not hold up under scrutiny. When students are challenged on their uncritical and superficial acceptance of the material, they begin to see how what they believe is sorely lacking in content, as well as application. Watson's concern, however, was not to debunk Maslow, Drucker or anyone else, but instead was to reflect on the implications of superficial learning in management training specifically and in the social sciences in general.

A much more critical approach to Maslow has been taken by Soper, Milford and Rosenthal (1995), in an article that shows that Maslow's approach to motivation has more status as a belief system or as a "religion" than it does as a scientific explanation of motivation. In fact, these researchers found it odd that a theory such as this, which has never been researched or supported by empirical facts, should hold sway over a discipline such as marketing for so long when it has so little credibility. Disciplines such as marketing, psychology and management take considerable pride in themselves because of their "scientific" approach to the facts in their respective fields. Nevertheless, they continue to embrace Maslow's theory of motivation despite its unreliability, dubiousness and undependability. In previous research (Maddock & Fulton, 1996), articles have been found that are theoretically and methodologically sound in their approach to leadership and other issues that will, at the same time, defeat and sabotage their own credibility by referring to Maslow's hierarchy as a basis for their whole approach. This was mentioned and a few sample articles were referred to in the introduction to this book.

MOTIVATION AS REWARD

According to Seligman (1991), the death knell to behaviorism was sounded in 1959 when Chomsky wrote his devastating critique of Skinner's book, *Verbal Behavior*. Because of this momentous event, the party—which for behaviorism lasted thirty-nine years—was over.

You would never know it. Clinicians in psychology and other disciplines still promote and endorse behavioristic methods of motivation, which by now are notoriously ineffective in many areas and only moderately effective in some other limited and restricted areas. For example, schools have found that the unwieldy requirement of behavior modification of documenting every behavior of a disruptive child is physically and economically impossible. Furthermore, methods such as reward, time-out, withholding punishment and schedules of reinforcement—all big tickets with those who promote reward theories of motivation—are ineffective with children who have attention deficit problems and other disruptive behaviors. The answer, according to most administrators and teachers, is medication, which then "motivates" the children in terms of controlling their behaviors. Not an ideal solution, but a necessary and effective one. This is because when one child is out of control, the whole class is out of control and no one learns anything. Medication has provided education with a solution and has also replaced the ineffective and outmoded "technology" of behavior modification.

Kohn (1993a, 1993b) exposed the ineffectiveness of rewards (and punishment) in two publications, one of which relates to the educational and school environment and the other to incentive plans and quotas in business. Kohn stated that there are at least seventy studies showing that extrinsic motivators, such as grades, praise, incentives, and the like, are not only ineffective over the long run but are generally counterproductive. This is because rewards detract from the natural tendency to learn, to achieve and to satisfy curiosity. In terms of education, Kohn found it astounding how many educators use the term *motivation* when what they really mean is control or compliance. The same is true in business and industry. Kohn also gave an example of how the reward of praise can backfire. For example, when a teacher singles out one student as a model of compliance and conformity, that student is often ridiculed and possibly even isolated by the other students in the class. This isolation is often the worst ridicule of all.

By far the largest body of knowledge that deals with rewards as motivators grows out of research with animals. It is a generally conceded conclusion, even by behaviorists, that animals do not have the same drives and needs as humans, except on a purely physical and reflexive level. As Seligman (1991) stated, "animal and human behavior are inadequately explained by drives and needs, and cognition (thinking) needs to be invoked in order to explain complex, higher level behavior" (p. 9).

One of the best applications of reward, with all of its complex schedules of reinforcement and various contingencies, is in the operation of slot machines in casinos. But even in this category, our own research has found that reward is not the motivation for visiting a casino and operating a slot machine. Instead, subjects we interviewed in a number of casino studies indicated that it was the escape and the disorientation—that "disconnection" from the outside world—that brought them to the casino. The potential for reward played a secondary role. This is the reason they keep going back even though they do not win large amounts of money— as many of them reported, "You win some and you lose some."

Motivation is not rewards and punishments.

MOTIVATION AS EMOTION

We are told by consultants, business leaders and government officials that emotion has no place in the day-to-day operation of business or in governmental organizations. And yet, emotions are an inseparable part of everyday life, both inside and outside of the work world. Anyone who has ever worked knows this. But despite a prevalence of emotion and the expression of emotion at work, research has basically overlooked emotion and has never even scratched the surface of emotional issues in the workplace. According to Ashworth (1995), despite the prevalence of emotion in the workplace, research has been generally confined to certain "acceptable" and relatively stable affective states, such as job satisfaction, mood and certain aspects of commitment, and the role of emotion in certain organizational events, such as in organizational change or "downsizing" or in isolated acts of violence that attract the attention of everyone.

Ashworth provided a comprehensive and extensive treatment of the subject of emotion in the workplace. His article consists of a complete review of emotion. It looks closely at the way that emotion and rationality are related to each other. It then looks at a historical perspective of dealing with emotion at work, describing the ways in which the emotions and the expression of emotions are regulated and controlled in most organizations. Then it shows how emotion is inextricably enmeshed in the workplace and at times can improve organizational effectiveness rather than undermining it. Ashworth's article is very bold, for it opens the door to an area that has been treated in a very limited and circumscribed way in the past, and that has been disguised, hidden, suppressed, buried, normalized, repressed and "swept under the carpet." Why? Because of a fear that it would disrupt the organization if exposed. Even the government has become involved with complex sets of regulations for sexual harassment that guard against the intrusion of emotion into the workplace, under the threat of heavy fines and even extended jail terms for those who offend.

MOTIVATION IS EMOTION, AND LEADERSHIP IS MOTIVATION

In the workplace, there is a tremendous opportunity to tap unused resources, which is one of the purposes of this book. These resources come through emotion, which already exists in the workplace but only in a very weak and disengendered way. The literature on motivation has been very limited, and according to Ashworth (1995) overly rational. Theories of emotion based on expectancy theory (Vroom, 1964) and behavior modification in organizations (Luthans & Kreitner, 1975) heavily rely on rational, logical and verbal processes and exclude emotion almost entirely.

Ashworth discussed unleashing the tremendous power of emotion that has been hidden in organizations, and using it in a constructive manner to energize people and to maximize motivation. The result is to get individuals cognitively, physically, affectively and personally engaged in their work, in the pursuit of a goal. Fine (1988) quoted a cook who spoke about the "high" that characterizes smooth performance: "I just love the activity. I concentrate so totally, that I don't know how I feel. It's like another sense takes over." Interestingly, frequent visitors to casinos reported the same thing about why they really go to casinos, after they get beyond the initial rationalization of expectancy (winning).

Ashworth (1995) concluded:

> The common theme underlying these perspectives is that strong motivation and psychological involvement are not possible without an emotional attachment to the work or work context. The traditional focus on effort (behavior) and expectations (cognition) addresses the hands and head of the individual, but not the heart. (p. 97)

The implications of the connections between emotions and motivations are seen in Bass' transformational leadership paradigm, but are not brought into a full operational understanding until it is seen within the context of our own theory of motivation and emotion, which has been worked out primarily with consumers in places and in events where they feel quite free to express their emotions.

THE ROLE OF PSYCHOLOGY AND PSYCHOLOGISTS IN LEADERSHIP

It was noted earlier that Seligman and others could clearly see that the era for behaviorism ended with the Chomsky-Skinner debates in 1959. But it wasn't that simple. What took place was a kind of metamorphosis, in which behavioristic psychologists became "cognitive" psychologists. A cognitive psychologist is one who looks inside of the black box and makes observations about what might be going on in the mind. As you may recall, behaviorists, in an effort to be pure scientists, eschewed anything mental or mentalistic. But as LeDoux (1996) has pointed out, cognitive psychology is even more of a sham. It is a sham because it ignores emotion and passion—the most vital parts of human existence. He states:

> Although this approach has had its share of successes, these have come at a high price. In trading in the passion of an emotion for thoughts about it, cognitive theories had turned emotions into cold, lifeless states of mind. Lacking sound and fury, emotions as cognition signify nothing, or at least nothing very emotional. Our emotions are full of blood, sweat and tears, but you wouldn't know it from examining modern cognitive research on emotion. (p. 42)

This is why managers, educators, marketers and others have looked to professional psychology for the answers and have not found any. Professional psychology was busily presenting itself as a "science," and in doing so completely overlooked human emotion as well as some other vital parts of human motivation that we will discuss in chapter 3. In a more careful analysis of this scenario, one might conclude that the profession of psychology has been more self-serving than it has been in serving the people who have looked to the profession for assistance.

LEADERSHIP = MOTIVATION = EMOTION

The formula Leadership = Motivation = Emotion has wide support in the literature, but has seldom been put into operation. This book and the treatment presented here do just that. It presents an operational approach to leadership.

Ashworth (1995) presented the background for this liaison among motivation, emotion and leadership:

> Leaders may persuade with logic, but they motivate through emotion. Leaders must come to grips with the challenges of emotion, a key driver of productivity, quality and other factors that lead to business success. The words "motivation," "emotion" and "motion" all derive from the same Latin root meaning "to move." When you want to motivate people to take action, engage their emotions. (p. 97)

Some empirical evidence is already provided for this assertion. Pool (1997) looked at the relationship between leadership, job satisfaction and motivation. Although job satisfaction was described by Ashworth as a superficial or "quasi"-emotional component, it is at least one ingredient of emotion. Job satisfaction is an attitude that individuals maintain about their job. In this study, which employed the responses on the MLQ as the dependent variable, the relationship between leadership style, work motivation and substitutes of leadership were examined in terms of their overall ability to predict job satisfaction. The results of both stepwise and independent analyses indicated that the most powerful predictor of job satisfaction for the population was work motivation, which explained 32.1 percent of the job satisfaction variance. Based on these findings, it was concluded that there was a positive relation between work motivation and job satisfaction, and as job satisfaction increases, work motivation also increases, and vice versa.

The motivational system that we have put together after years of research has paid off in consumer psychology. We have been able to save dying brands and products. We have established discernible differences in commodity products such as banks and hospitals, so that consumers could recognize them as unique and different from other commodity products or services. We have found the hot buttons that brought consumers back to a product or service that was failing. All because we have come to understand what motivates people.

The same thing applies in the field of leadership. The leader is just another individual, as Clinton and O. J. Simpson have proven. They put their pants on just like the rest of us do. They have both good and bad traits. From time to time, when things are going badly, their old character traits slip through and they become irritable, angry, irrational and capricious. They behave in immature ways. They exhibit traits that amaze us, and we say, "I always thought of him/her as a leader! What's going on?" They disappoint us.

But when we see the leader as both human and as a motivator, we begin to understand. The motivational structure that we have put together in the last twenty-five years of research is now serving in the form of an atlas, or a road map, which guides our way into the minds of those that we are charged with leading and directing. This becomes quite clear as this book unfolds and addresses the problems that our leaders confront every day, motive by motive by motive.

MOTIVATION AND TRANSFORMATIONAL LEADERSHIP

The discussion of the close relationship between emotion, motivation and leadership provides a smooth transition into the areas of transformational leadership (Bass, 1985, 1997; Bycio, Hackett & Allen, 1995).

By way of factor analysis, Bass (1997) found five factors involved in leadership. Two of them are referred to as transactional, and three as transformational. The transactional leader relies more on rational and logical thinking and free exchange of work in return for extrinsic rewards such as pay, vacations, hospitalization, and so on. Conversely, the transformational leader emphasizes the intrinsic value of effort and maximizes it in terms of organizational goals and events, by articulating a coherent, futuristic vision—one that is compelling and commanding, but also intrinsically rewarding. These goals and values are not only intrinsic, they are transcendental and translational. Basically, they point toward a better future, meaningful goals and the feeling that one is doing something significant and important in terms of one's work.

Generally, the literature on transformational leadership has demonstrated high job satisfaction, satisfaction with corporate leadership, leader effectiveness, stimulation and the willingness to engage in extra effort without any extrinsic reward. The company itself sets high goals, and then the employees as part of that company all strive to do the best they can in the achievement of these goals so that, as part of that company, they share in the rewards and in the harvest and the bounty when it comes. This type of commitment is often seen in police and fire organizations, where people who work for relatively low pay rates are willing to risk their lives for their job. This is evidenced at Parris Island, South Carolina, where a self-centered, narcissistic and conceited high school graduate, who is interested only in himself, in a matter of six weeks, is turned into a Marine; a Marine who not only has a new sense of pride, but is willing to die for his country. When the whole process is considered, it is nothing short of amazing.

There are many examples of transformational leadership in organizations such as those just mentioned where there are no extrinsic rewards whatsoever: in churches and religious organizations, professional and college athletic teams (particularly basketball and football), community organizations, multilevel sales groups, associations, unions and so forth. These organizations have nothing to work with other than emotion. They often have leaders who are charismatic, magnetic and charming. But this can often cause other problems that are also discussed here.

Our analysis of transformational leadership goes beyond that presented in the present literature because it involves an in-depth analysis of the emotion that is involved; not only in organizations but also in leadership per se, wherever it is seen or played out. It extends well beyond behavior modification or beyond the humanism endorsed by Maslow. Succinctly and briefly, it consists of emotion, which appears to be the buried treasure in every organization, regardless of its overall goal, mission or assignment.

Leadership = Motivation = Emotion.

REFERENCES

Ashworth, B. E. (1995). Emotion in the workplace: A reappraisal. *Human Relations 48*(2), 97.

Bass, B. (1985). *Leadership and performance beyond expectations.* New York: The Free Press.

Bass, B. (1997). Does the transactional–transformational leadership paradigm transcend organizational and national boundaries? *American Psychologist 52*(2), 130–139.

Bycio, P., Hackett, R. D., & Allen, J. S. (1995). Further assessments of Bass's (1985) conceptualization of transactional and transformational leadership. *Journal of Applied Psychology 80*(4), 468–478.

Filson, B. (1994, September). The new leadership: Health-care leaders should provide motivation for change. *Hospitals and Health Networks 68*(17), 76.

Fine, G. A. (1988). Letting off steam? Redefining a restaurant's work environment. In M. D. Moore & R. C. Snyder (Eds.), *Inside organizations: Understanding the human dimension* (pp. 119–128). Newbury Park, CA: Sage Publishers.

Hallam, G. L., & Campbell, D. P. (1992, May). *Selecting team members? Start with a theory of team effectiveness.* Paper presented at the seventh annual meeting of the Society of Industrial and Organizational Psychology, Montreal, Quebec, Canada.

Helton, S. (1997). Leadership for a new age. *Nation's Business 85*(5), 18.

Hogan, R., Curphy, G. J., & Hogan, J. (1994). What we know about leadership. *American Psychologist 49*(6), 493–504.

Jones, E. (1955). *The life and work of Sigmund Freud* (Vol. 2). New York: Basic Books.

Kohn, A. (1993a). *Punished by rewards.* Boston: Houghton-Mifflin.

Kohn, A. (1993b, September-October). Why incentive plans cannot work. *Harvard Business Review 71*, 54–63.

LeDoux, J. E. (1996). *The emotional brain: The mysterious underpinnings of emotional life.* New York: Simon and Schuster.

Lucia, A. (1997). Leaders know how to listen. *HR Focus 74*(4), 25.

Luthans, F., & Kreitner, R. (1975). *Organizational behavior modification.* Glenview, IL: Scott, Foresman.

Maddock, R. C., & Fulton, R. L. (1996). *Marketing to the mind: Right brain strategies in advertising and marketing.* Westport, CT: Quorum Books.

Maslow, A. H. (1970). *Motivation and personality* (2nd ed.). New York: Harper & Row.

Milliken, W. F. (1996, October). The Eastman way. *Quality Progress.*

Pool, S. W. (1997). The relationship of job satisfaction with substitutes of leadership, leadership behavior and work motivation. *Journal of Psychology 131*(3), 271.

Seligman, M. E. P. (1991). *Learned optimism.* New York: Alfred A. Knopf.

Shapiro, D. H., Schwartz, C. E., & Astin, J. (1996). Controlling ourselves, controlling our world: Psychology's role in understanding positive and negative consequences of seeking and gaining control. *American Psychologist 51*(12) 1213–1230.

Soper, B., Milford, G. E., & Rosenthal, G. T. (1995). Belief when evidence does not support the theory. *Psychology and Marketing 12*(5), 415–422.

Vroom, V. H. (1964). *Work and motivation.* New York: Wiley.

Watson, T. J. (1996). Motivation: That's Maslow, Isn't it? *Management Learning 27*(4), 447.

Chapter 3

The Silent Side of Human Motivation

Breakthroughs in motivation have been depressingly few and far between. Psychologists and psychiatrists have never given executives, managers or leaders the practical information they need to understand how the human mind functions. They have never given them what they need to know about the origins of behavior. Laymen everywhere are at a similar disadvantage. If you have ever taken a psychology course, you have probably noticed that much of what is studied does not apply to everyday human affairs. And courses in management also leave a lot to be desired.

The chief reason that academic psychology does not translate into practical breakthroughs is that it is academic. Psychologists and psychiatrists study people in laboratories, professional offices, patient treatment centers and campus facilities. The wisdom they impart to business and laypeople is derived from those artificial conditions. Hence, a lot of the wisdom is also artificial.

The conclusions here are the results of years of organizational and clinical research. We believe we have made a breakthrough in understanding—a virtual restructuring of the nonconscious mind. The practical payoff for leaders and managers is the insight we provide about human behavior—that long-awaited practical breakthrough. The breakthrough is not derived from accepted academic wisdom. We have studied employees and middle and upper management at the source: where they work, where they earn their money and where they spend their time. There's a difference.

Another difference is the method we used to get to the heart of the matter, which is a departure from standard diagnostic surveys. The

Table 3.1
Categories of the Human Mind

	What You See	**What You Don't See**
What Others See	**OPEN AREA** Logic Explanations Shared Reality	**BLIND SPOT** Rationalizations Excuses Justifications
What Others Don't See	**SECRETS** **?**	**SILENT SIDE** Motives Emotions Passion

method involves closing one's eyes and visualizing the issues, rather than just verbalizing and talking about them. Through guided imagery, respondents are introduced to their nonconscious minds, which think in terms of pictures rather than words. This methodology has been successful in getting into nonconscious imagery, helping us to derive the "map" or "atlas" of motives that make up most of the nonconscious mind. These motives are discussed in this chapter.

FINDING NONCONSCIOUS MOTIVES

The contents of the human mind comprise four categories as seen in Table 3.1. Two are perceptible to outsiders: the open category, which includes logic, explanations and experiences shared with others; and the blind spot category, of which you are not aware but others are. This blind spot consists of rationalizations, excuses and self-justifications.

A third category consists of things only you know about: secrets that remain hidden from outsiders and that no one can see.

The fourth category is what we refer to as the *Silent Side*. The

Silent Side consists of things neither you nor outsiders detect: the motives and the emotions that cause people to behave in the way they do.

Leadership needs to be concerned with the Silent Side quadrant. Although its content is not apparent to you or to outsiders, the Silent Side is where most major decisions are made. In fact, it is where almost all decisions are made.

THE STRUCTURE OF HUMAN MOTIVATION

Because the nonconscious mind is simple and straightforward and not complex or devious, it has a limited number of motives. We have detected eleven, which fit into five categories. These categories exist in every human being, and they account for most all human behavior, consumer or otherwise. They are:

1. Orientation
2. Survival
3. Adaptation
4. Expectation
5. Play

Do these motivations vary with individual differences? Very little, if at all. Factors such as race, IQ, weight or achievement have a minimal impact on the nonconscious mind. For the purposes of consumer sampling, variations are negligible, except when it comes to gender. Major differences between male and female nonconscious motivators have been found in our research, and they become more obvious as this part of the mind is opened up to you in this chapter.

We have verified the existence of the motives we describe using the traditional research technique of factor analysis. Our method and results are described in chapter 5.

The emotional drivers of the nonconscious must be understood because they are vital components of decision making. We repeat, leadership is motivation; the leader is a motivator. And Leadership = Motivation = Emotion. And if A = B and B = C, then A = C.

THE ORIENTATION MOTIVES: PERSONAL, PLACE, TIME AND CIRCUMSTANTIAL

Much as a migrating bird's internal compass keeps it on a steady course when it flies north in the summer and south in the winter,

Orientation Motives permit individuals to keep their bearings while dealing day to day with external realities and stresses.

Orientation is as integral to the nonconscious mind as the heartbeat is to the chest cavity. And like the heartbeat, the Orientation Motives do not usually engage our conscious attention. Someone under stress saying, "I don't want to lose it," or encountering a severe case of Alzheimer's disease and saying "I hope I don't live that long," are acknowledgments of the existence of the Orientation Motives.

There are four Orientation Motives:

Personal Orientation

Place Orientation

Time Orientation

Circumstantial Orientation

These four Orientation Motives can be ranked in order of importance because they break down successively when disorientation occurs. The most fragile is circumstantial orientation, which is the first to go. Time orientation, a stronger impulse, goes next. Place orientation, stronger yet, is more resistant to breakdown. Personal orientation, the strongest of all, is most deeply entrenched, and the last to disappear when a person becomes disoriented.

Personal orientation gives you your sense of self and what you stand for. Much of what we refer to here as the Personal Orientation Motive consists of self-control. Personal orientation is the nerve center for self-control. Even in a strange, disorienting dream, personal orientation almost always remains intact. In other words, you may be in a place where you lived many years ago, with people who are long since deceased, but you remain essentially the same person—the person that you are in everyday life. For obvious reasons, personal orientation is always a factor in any leadership decision.

Place, which is the second strongest Orientation Motive, is less rigid. Its temporary loss, as in jet lag, can be unsettling, but a gradual shift of place orientation is easily accommodated. For example, when walking from the daylight into a darkened movie theater, or vice versa, a transition occurs in place orientation. In fact, a controlled change of place orientation can be downright pleasurable; otherwise, people would not take vacations. It is rumored that Henry Ford had this in mind when he gave his reasons for entering the car business: "Everybody wants to get where they ain't, and when they get there they want to get back home again." This is another way of saying that people want to disconnect for awhile, and then reconnect.

Time orientation is that sense we all possess of the approximate date and hour. It is not nearly as strong as personal and place orientation. Accordingly, when we become engrossed in some interesting activity, we lose track of time. Likewise, after a dream in which past and present have been blurred, time orientation is sometimes confused. Among elderly people, time orientation can be severely and permanently destroyed as brain deterioration damages the internal clock. One example of time orientation is music, where it is usually the beat that has the appeal and will increase memory of an advertisement or a product, or in some cases even increase productivity.

But time is a constraint we all like to escape now and then. In fact, the fun of doing so has generated whole industries: theme parks, resorts and restaurants whose settings create the feel of past or future times. Conversely, the desire to escape this boundary is often seen in tardiness, absenteeism, daydreaming or other "timeless" activities that interfere directly and indirectly with "real time."

Circumstantial orientation supplements the time sense by signaling whether it's a good or bad day. It is a composite of impressions about health, income, domestic life, expectations and other variables that affect the present. Because of its transient character, circumstantial is the Orientation Motive most susceptible to change. Think of all the people who have a couple of drinks after work to forget the day's cares, or the recent mania for virtual-reality games that seem to put the player into a whole new situation or circumstance without ever leaving the living room.

Orientation Motives and Human Behavior

Through our research, we have determined that although people do not want to lose their orientation altogether, they do seek to change it temporarily. That explains a great deal about human behavior, especially when it comes to recreational and discretionary spending. In short, people want to disconnect, and then to reconnect. That's what vacations and days off are all about. A problem arises when individuals, despite their use (or misuse) of generous vacation and holiday leave and free weekends, continue to disorient or disconnect during times when they should be working. For example: A salesman who traveled extensively loved his work because he was always on the road meeting new people. He was disconnected from home, kids, family and the home office. The problem was that he was so disconnected, and he enjoyed "visiting" with old customers and new prospects so thoroughly that he never got down to the purpose of his journey, which was to sell. After a two-year decline in sales commissions, he still did not get the message and eventually had to be terminated.

In our effort to get away from "artificial populations" (students, patients, etc.), much of our research has been with consumers. We like to do research with people where they spend their money in their off time because that's the real determinant behind motivation. They are doing what they want to do, on their own time and with their own money. During our investigation of entertainment preferences, we visited a number of theme parks. In the line of duty, we tried out dozens of "thrill rides," and we can assure you that they really deliver the thrills. Perhaps you've also felt the temporary disorientation that comes from whirling, climbing, dropping, splashing, submerging and plunging into total darkness. Fun, right? If you don't think so, you're definitely not a teenager.

In terms of consumer demographics, teenagers constitute a distinct group of paying thrill seekers. As an age group, they are the most confused about personal orientation. Because of their adolescent identity confusion, they go for theme park rides that disorient and reorient their sense of personal identity.

It may be that you're part of the demographic group that prefers a sedate theme park with an old-time setting. Such a choice provides a temporary adjustment of your time and place orientations. During your visit, as you watch traditional crafts being demonstrated—blacksmithing or hand looming, for example—you forget your everyday concerns and, for a while, experience life as it was in an earlier era. It's all a pleasant, momentary alteration of your circumstantial orientation as well as orientation to time and place. Would you like to hold on to that disorienting experience for awhile? Buy a coffee cup, a tee shirt or a cap and take it home with you. It really doesn't prolong the experience when you're back in reality again, but it does *seem* to prolong it.

Had a humdrum day? One antidote is a good meal in an upscale restaurant. But there's more to fine dining than tasty food and a good menu. If the restaurant decor is distinctive, dining out will invoke a pleasant change in your place orientation. And suppose that upon arriving you're greeted and waited on by a solicitous staff that has been trained to treat you as if you're special. Perhaps they've even taken the mega-memory course and greet you by name! You're soon enjoying a brief, positive change in your personal orientation. Good restaurants that understand and cater to the need for a change in personal and place orientation do much better than good restaurants that do not.

People who say that clothes don't define the person are only partly right. Wardrobe is a means of stating personal orientation. The statement you make, of course, varies according to circumstances, so you probably keep various styles of clothes handy. It's not unusual, particularly during a period of mental depression, for someone to go out and buy several different outfits, hoping to change personal orientation from upsettingly old hat to refreshingly new.

Cosmetics add another dimension to personal orientation. For instance, during my morning drive to work, I never cease to be amazed at the number of female commuters fixating on their rear-view mirrors, risking life and limb (mine included) as they apply makeup in traffic. Many of these working professionals cover the last few yards to the office in running shoes, their pumps stashed in a shoulder bag. These are people whose personal orientation at work is much different than at home. Their complex, dangerous morning ritual demonstrates the importance they attach to both in that transition between places: home and work.

These examples were chosen for their simplicity, so they are probably not very surprising. Surprising or not, the orientation implications of each have been confirmed by research. Clearly, orientation factors play a role in every consumer decision, simple or complex. Advertisers and marketers must therefore take them into account.

THE SURVIVAL MOTIVES: SPIRITUAL, PHYSICAL, TERRITORIAL AND SEXUAL

Like Orientation Motives, the Survival Motives operate nonconsciously. They reveal themselves only when they are threatened by an outside source.

The four Survival Motives, listed in order of importance, are:

Spiritual

Physical

Territorial

Sexual

The Importance of the Spiritual Survival Motive

Spiritual survival is the most important Survival Motive, and one of the two major motives that surfaced in our research (see chapter 8). Furthermore, spiritual survival and personal orientation are the most powerful, dominant and forceful of all Silent Side motives. Rec-

ognizing the importance of the Spiritual Survival Motive is fundamental to understanding the Silent Side of the nonconscious mind.
Because its importance has been misunderstood to date, spiritual
survival must be explained in some detail.

Let's be clear about the term *spiritual*. It does not denote a
churchly or religious sector of the Silent Side. It denotes a striving
for something beyond physical existence; values and beliefs that
transcend the mortal world and live on after us. Spiritual survival
refers to whatever people are passionate about!

In the spring of 1997, more than six hundred homes along the
Ohio River were under six feet of water. Many of those people left
their homes—under water—in order to go to Memphis and watch
Kentucky play basketball in the SEC playoffs. Is that passion? Now,
what's more important: spiritual survival or basic shelter?

A golf aficionado described his annual "pilgrimage" to the Masters
at Augusta. He said "It is my one totally fulfilling spiritual experience of the year."

Paul Fleischman, a psychiatrist and author whose work on spiritual survival is introduced in this chapter, told us after he read our
manuscript, "I've always known that something besides baseball
was going on out there at Fenway Park!"

Spiritual survival's preeminence as a motivator does not square
with the celebrated work of Maslow, whose views on the hierarchy
of human needs have been gospel for psychologists and business
consultants for decades. According to Maslow (1970), individuals
strive to meet a graduated set of needs, moving from the basic
to the increasingly sophisticated as those needs are successively
gratified. Physical survival is the first and foremost need, according to Maslow. Spiritual concerns (which Maslow labeled *self-
actualization*) become important only after basic physical needs are
met. In other words, if you're hungry and cold, spiritual survival is
the last thing on your mind.

Our investigations indicate otherwise. Spiritual survival comes
first and foremost, ranking second only to personal orientation. And
that fact has a huge impact on consumer decisions. Because it is
an abstract motive, spiritual survival is difficult to describe. But it
exists in all of us, beginning with early childhood.

Using our visualization method, we found that almost everyone,
before the age of seven, has had an experience with death or dying.
Perhaps a relative or friend passed away. Perhaps a pet died. Whatever their origin, early experiences with death have an enormous,
permanent impact on the Silent Side of the nonconscious mind.
Being led to a casket to view a deceased loved one, or watching a
burial, or simply seeing for the first time an animal's lifeless carcass,

is the most profound experience of childhood. It may soon be discarded by the conscious mind, but its vestiges remain embedded in the Silent Side.

What conclusions do children draw from death experiences? They conclude that life is fragile and impermanent but that there is something that outlasts death: the life of the spirit. That conclusion allows them to mock physical death during play. Halloween—which is rapidly becoming our nation's second largest holiday—is all about a spoof on death and dying, particularly for children. But underneath the mockery is a reverence—a need—for spiritual survival.

As individuals age, this spiritual conviction does not diminish, although it may have been plastered over with logical, rational, "loud side" thinking. A mature person may rationally dismiss the notion of spiritual survival; but deep in the Silent Side, that motive is alive and well. Individuals can be trained to accept loss of life (it happens to every U.S. Marine recruit who survives boot camp), as long as physical death serves a surviving spiritual goal such as patriotism. Every community has cherished examples of heroes who, in emergency situations, chose physical death over a spiritual one. Examples are seen weekly on *Rescue 911* on television. Deep down, everyone affirms that a spiritual death is far worse than a physical one. It is ultimately unthinkable.

Components of the Spiritual Survival Motive

Spiritual survival embodies more than religious feelings. In *The Healing Spirit: Explorations into Religion and Psychiatry* (1990), Paul R. Fleischman, a psychiatrist, maintained that many conventional religions have not succeeded in resolving personal dilemmas. As a result, people adopt other spiritual pursuits, including beliefs in a caring higher power, the sanctity of the individual, the transcendence of the community, the endurance of human love, the eternal virtue of self-sacrifice, the beauty of inner peace and the quest for meaning in one's work. The most important aspect of spiritual survival is human love in all its manifestations: love of country, love of family, brotherly love, sexual love and love of those less fortunate. All of these aspects create in each individual a need to be right, to approach perfection, to acquire wisdom, to speak the truth and to be consistent.

Fleischman had completed more than twenty years of cross-cultural research in which he examined many of the world's religions and found ten common elements in spirituality. These elements are extremely useful in arriving at an operational definition of spirituality. Operational definitions eliminate much of the

Table 3.2
Fleischman's Table of Elements Critical in Spiritual Survival

ELEMENT	DESCRIPTION
Witness Significance	Belief that a higher power listens, sees and understands
Lawful Order	Belief in the basic order of the universe and the world in which we live
Wholeness	Involves affirmation and acceptance of the person
A Sense of Calling	A universal need for importance; to feel like one's work and life are relevant, connected
Membership	Part of a larger network that affirms, accepts and legitimizes the person and his or her beliefs
Release	Renewal and release of new power
Human Love	A vital element: love, bonding and marriage overcome fear, pain and loss; also includes patriotism and love of country
Sacrifice	The ability to go beyond one's self; often used to "bargain" with a higher power
Meaningful Death	The goal of any spiritual program, organized or unorganized
Inner Peace	Translating self-centeredness, worry and responsibility into peace

confusion regarding agreement, especially in highly passionate (and therefore disputable and controversial) areas such as spirituality. These elements are found in Table 3.2.

Most of today's movies and made-for-TV dramas are written around a central theme of spiritual survival—right versus wrong—with eventual resolution in favor of right. It is a format everyone intuitively understands. On a day-to-day basis, people act on their Spiritual Survival Motive by doing what they believe is right, which is not always easy. But doing otherwise causes feelings of guilt and noxious whiffs of spiritual death, which are far less preferable.

By now you are probably wondering how all this relates to human behavior as a fundamental driver—particularly in an organization or in the workplace. Because all individuals are motivated by spiritual survival, they perpetually strive to make what they believe are the right decisions and the correct judgments. That is a much different thing from Maslow's celebrated conclusion that people are motivated by spiritual concerns only after they have overcome life's physical challenges. Every manager, or anyone who has been in a leadership position, already has intuited this fact, even if they don't actively know it.

The Role of Spiritual Survival in Advertising

The problem with spiritual survival is that it is an abstract concept and difficult to understand. But examples will usually overcome those barriers to understanding. Perhaps the best examples come from advertising because its main idea is to motivate people. The ads referred to here are not only some of the most motivational ads ever written or produced, but also (and not accidentally) have been around the longest.

DeBeers' powerful, never-changing message that "a diamond is forever" strikes a spiritual note. DeBeers' advertising, in fact, aims exclusively at spiritual survival; particularly with the message of "forever." One critical aspect of spiritual survival is the aspect of the eternal, the infinite or the perpetual. Just like the product itself, DeBeers' message of the infinite is itself perpetual. It never changes.

Not that it is always easy to foresee how a product will relate to the Spiritual Survival Motive. People sometimes distort the notion of what is right, associating it with words like "clean" and "pure." The following examples, reported by a retired Procter & Gamble executive, illustrate how such notions can get out of hand. Procter & Gamble received frequent letters from consumers reporting they ate Ivory Soap because it was advertised as being "ninety-nine and forty-four one-hundreths percent pure." Occasionally the company was named in lawsuits brought by consumers who practiced home chemistry with various cleaning products. Unsatisfied with the cleaning power of one product, they would mix several, often with results that were literally explosive.

As Procter & Gamble discovered, a consumer's quest for pure perfection can go to extremes. So can the need to be in the right, which often unleashes enormous passion. A case in point is the National Rifle Association, whose much advertised position on gun control is deemed by many to distort the intent of the U.S. Constitution and bears the marks of a passionate crusade.

Michelin does not simply harp on the technical features of its tires, it focuses on "what is riding on your tires," that is, safety, security, family values, and parental responsibility. Few products are more mundane than tires, but Michelin is quite savvy about the spiritual component of every consumer decision.

Serta never shows a mattress in its television ads. The ads simply show a little boy going to sleep in a peaceful, pastoral scene. Meanwhile, the competition, Simmons and Sealy, show the springs, padding, flexibility and firmness. But Serta has discovered that potential mattress buyers are not interested in what makes a mattress. They are instead interested in its inner peace (see Table 3.2)—another element of the Spiritual Survival Motive.

For years, although its cars were by no means top of the line in fit, finish, or sophistication, Cadillac used the spiritual approach, persuading people that they were buying more than a mere automobile. Today, with cars that are competitively high tech, Cadillac ads still talk of more than engineering. Now they talk of "creating a higher standard," of perfectionism, achievement, enduring quality, of spiritual survival! The latest Cadillac TV spot concludes when a trusting tot gleefully jumps into daddy's waiting arms.

McDonald's, unlike Burger King, Wendy's, and other competitors, does not simply sell fast food. It sells values and principles, emphasizing that a trip to the golden arches is a proper family outing—the right thing to do. By marketing directly to children, who will take the message to their parents, McDonald's underscores the spiritual component of its message.

Hamburgers can be spiritual. Given the realities of competition and the Silent Side, hamburgers must be spiritual. Failure to take the kids on a trip to McDonald's can often result in a parental guilt trip. Just as human love is one of the integral positive components of spiritual survival, guilt is one of the negative components of spiritual survival.

Spiritual Survival as a Motive in Organizations

In many cases of organizations, problems can be more easily recognized and solved if the causes are known. That goes without saying. But at times, the spiritual issues are elusive and poorly defined, thus remaining unresolved. For example, let's use the salesman discussed earlier—the one who loved to be on the road.

Employees who are separated from the home office day after day and week after week often lose their loyalty to the organization. Loyalty and fidelity are elements of spiritual survival (see Table 3.2). An individual who functions as a salesperson and an account representative and who spends most of his or her time away from the home office can easily become detached or disconnected from the organization. This person loses a sense of belonging and allegiance. Therefore, when something goes wrong at the home office and he or she is called on by the customer to explain the snafu, the employee sides with the client and not with the organization. He or she might say things like "Those people back there don't know what they are doing," or "They are so screwed up in that plant that it's a wonder they ever get the work out." In this case the account representative, in siding with the customer, is eroding the customer's confidence in the organization by communicating disloyalty and disaffiliation. The end result is that the account representative also loses the customer, the customer's business and his or her commission for renewed business in the years to come.

The Physical Survival Motive in Organizations

The Physical Survival Motive is obvious and consists of three elements: food, air and water. Maslow believed it was the basic building block in the pyramid. To us, it is basic but not as important as you may think because people do things that are counterproductive to their physical survival, even though they know better. For example, at least one tobacco company (Phillip Morris) has admitted that smoking can hasten or potentiate death. But that admission has essentially had a negligible effect on consumers' consumption of cigarettes.

As seen here, cigarette smoking is potentiated by the Adaptation Motive, which is the motive to do what other people do and to be like them. Believe it or not, this motive can be stronger and more vigorous and potent than the motive of physical survival. It also explains other phenomena such as drug abuse, alcohol abuse, and so on. If physical survival is the most important motive, why would people do things to undermine their own physical survival? There must be motives that are stronger, which emphasizes how off base Maslow really was.

Most people go to work every day to sustain the Physical Survival Motive. Because it is a strong motive, it should be sufficient to make certain that people do come to work and do what they are supposed to do. But it doesn't do that. This is one of the reasons that, in the case of sales managers, we have to hire and pay a salary to adults (sales managers) so they can tell other grown adults (salespeople) to sell. It should be apparent, but it is not. One reason is because the Physical Survival Motive is low key, and is often taken for granted. As a result, people who come to work every day, day after day, often lose focus about what work is supposed to be, and why. It's because they lose contact with and lose focus of the Physical Survival Motive.

Like the other Silent Side motives, physical survival becomes aroused when it is threatened. The spread of crime is just one of many current issues that arouse this motive. We are increasingly aware that the natural environment, once taken for granted, is in jeopardy. The very food we eat, which once symbolized progress and security, is now suspect because of possibly unhealthful ingredients. Homeless people, obviously living on the edge of physical survival, literally stare us in the face. Basic health care is now up for grabs. We now know that diet and exercise do affect our lives, and how long we live and under what conditions. Physical survival is more of an issue than ever before.

Because most people tend to lose sight of the importance of the Physical Survival Motive, the effective leader needs to continually remind them of why they are working. Something as simple as this cannot be taken for granted. The effective leader needs to continually direct their attention toward this most important motive so that they can stay "in focus." Otherwise, regardless of the importance of this motive, people will lose sight of it. And if people lose sight of their motives, they eventually lose sight of their purpose and goals.

Advertising, Marketing and Territorial Survival

The appearance of Desmond Morris' (1967) bestseller *The Naked Ape* provided an amusing, persuasive argument that the territorial drives in animal species extend to organized human society. Silent Side diagnostics confirm this conclusion. In fact, territorial survival is one of the most powerful motives of the human nonconscious. Take, for example, an all-around good guy with a sweet personality who turns into the town crank whenever someone traipses across his lawn. The same reactions can be seen on a figurative basis in the business world. A corporate executive whose domain is challenged by company restructuring may react quite irrationally, possibly even deviously, to thwart the perceived invasion. Territoriality and the Territorial Survival Motive is a major factor in office politics.

Territoriality is a universal Silent Side motivation, but its exact nature is still clouded by cultural bias and sexism. Until lately, many believed that territorial survival was peculiar to men, not women. That mistaken conclusion was based on the aggressive behavior of males who dominated competitive occupations. Now that occupational barriers to women have lessened, females with professional careers exhibit the same Territorial Survival Motive as their male counterparts.

Territorial survival is more conspicuous than most Silent Side motives because it is regularly challenged by external forces. When his or her space is threatened, an individual usually reacts vigorously, displaying fear, anxiety or agitation. The resources at hand are mobilized to stop the incursion and often to reverse the process. In business this is called the *competitive spirit*. Some have even observed that the defensive tactics used in competition are the same as those used in war.

Because there is obviously a relation between territoriality and competition, further exploration of the Territorial Survival Motive may enhance understanding of competitiveness as a social phenomenon. Is there perhaps a parallel between childhood training and adult territorial competitiveness? The appeal of organized sports revolves around the Territorial Survival Motive. From early childhood, we all learn the importance of protecting a piece of turf with teamwork. That's not all there is to organized sports, of course. If you're a fan, you know how the ballyhoo, ritual and general hysteria surrounding championship teams transcends territoriality and enters the realm of the spiritual. Ever experienced depression the day after your team lost a game? If so, you're spiritually hooked.

The Olympic Games is a sporting event that invariably shifts motives from Territorial to Spiritual Survival Motive by interjecting elements of patriotism and nationalism. An extreme case was the 1994 Winter Olympics in Norway, during which untold millions watched the figure skating showdown between Nancy Kerrigan and Tonya Harding, both Americans. Territorial Survival Motives were altogether forgotten. Top-level, good versus bad, Spiritual Survival Motives had totally taken over.

In the late 1990s, there is much public debate about media violence and its effect on children. It is too early to make a definitive statement about this, but it could be that much of the aggression displayed by today's media-saturated kids is rooted in territorial emotions. So much of children's TV and children's electronic games is structured around aggressive competition: violent struggles of opposing forces, bash-and-crash attack and defense, threats to security that are dealt with by super heroes, super bunnies, super robots or whatever. Do such motifs twiddle children's inherent territorial emotions? Is there a long-term effect on kids? Someday we may know the answers.

Advertising, Marketing and Sexual Survival

It may come as a surprise to many, but the Sexual Survival Motive is the least powerful of the survival group. The motive is of course present in everyone, but its character varies considerably between males and females.

Sexual survival has four parts: gender, impulse, inhibition (females) and impotence (males). Generally speaking, the gender component is distinct: Motives are dramatically different between the genders. Impulse, the disposition toward quick, uninhibited action, is preponderantly male. Inhibition, a more cautious, deliberative, passive state, is overwhelmingly female. But there are also impulsive women and impotent men. Most people would prefer to have neither one of these personality styles as their leader.

The often stated cliché about the gulf between the genders is true. The other often stated cliché, which says that men tolerate love so they can get sex while women tolerate sex so they can get love is an overstatement, but only an overstatement. Although it may be politically incorrect, Silent Side research confirms that males are sexually preoccupied with virility, potency, masculinity, and aggression. Females are inclined to be more passive, acquiescent, compliant and submissive—at least for the moment.

Unlike many other aspects of consumer motivation, marketers seem to have a practical grasp of these differences, which they reinforce with their advertising. So it is that products such as pickup trucks, cowboy hats, and guns are pitched exclusively at males. And the pitch is usually toward impulse, which is a strong component of male sexual survival. When Ford introduced the Mustang in the mid 1960s, the ads read, "We made it hot, you make it scream." Picturing an in-charge male standing proudly by a car with a gorgeous female provocatively draped over it is another example of sexual survival marketing that hits male impulse. (And if you think these ads are out of style, check out the latest car magazines!) Sexual impulse is the mainstay of marketing to males in almost any area, but particularly when the product has something to do with performance.

Conversely, items such as flowers, costume jewelry, fragrances and weight loss programs are presumed to be female markets and are therefore marketed to inhibition. Jontue perfume, for example, describes itself as "Sensual . . . but not too far from innocence." In that phrase, the word "but" negates the impulsive connotation of "sensual"; "not too far from innocence" targets female inhibition. In a similar approach, Maybelline's ads whisper "Maybe she's born with it. . . . Maybe it's Maybelline." Inhibition is the mainstay of marketing to females—at least at the level of sexual survival.

There are a few noteworthy exceptions to the impulse–inhibition rule. Lingerie is customarily marketed to women directly at the level of sexual impulse. Diamonds are always marketed at the level of spiritual survival. And a recent Hyundai TV spot pulled a switcheroo that really clobbered accepted paradigms. In this ad, four women, noses pressed to an office window, drool over a shirt-less male hunk leaning on the hood of a Hyundai. "I wonder what he has under his hood?" one asks.

That ad sold Hyundais, which strongly suggests that the gulf between male and female Sexual Survival Motives is at least partly cultural and therefore subject to change. If Hyundai is right, change is upon us.

THE ADAPTATION MOTIVE

The first two groups of Silent Side Motives—Orientation and Survival—are acquired characteristics. Infants do not come into the world with a preprogrammed sense of person, place, time or circumstances. Likewise, they do not come hard-wired for spiritual, physical, territorial, and sexual survival. Those elements take time and development.

The Adaptation Motive is different: It predates birth. Ultrasound pictures of unborn babies clearly reveal movements of the hands to the face. Such movements aid the infant in adapting to the uterine environment. Fittingly, they are called *adaptors*.

Adaptors are extremely forceful and robust. After birth, and throughout life, they surface during moments of tension as an individual tries to cope with a challenging environment. The hand-to-face movement is recognizable in a child's thumb sucking, a reflex that is hard to break. The same movement is also apparent in adult cigarette smoking, a reflex that is even harder to break. Adaptation habits are never in fact broken. They may go into remission, but they can always reawaken.

The Adaptation Motive undergoes change during childhood, developing into an urge to be like everyone else. Preadolescent boys naturally congregate with other boys, and girls stick with girls, because kids want to be like their friends. Later, the Adaptation Motive grows stronger, which partly explains such peer-related phenomena as smoking, dressing similarly, making the high school honor roll, abusing drugs, or joining an athletic team. Adaptation works automatically on the Silent Side until it is threatened from outside. We have all seen cases of slavish adolescent conformity in which "everyone else" turned out to be the wrong crowd, requiring parents and police to take counteractive measures. Such cases are grim reminders of the power of the Adaptation Motive.

So powerful is this motive that it takes precedence over physical survival. Hard to believe? Maybe. But it explains why teenagers take up smoking to be like their friends even though they know the habit will threaten their physical survival.

Marketers have always understood the urge to conform, and campaigns pitched to that motive are as old as advertising. In common parlance, such approaches are known as "keeping up with the Joneses." Adaptation-based marketing was especially widespread during the 1950s and '60s when every house on the block was supposed to have the requisite number of labor-saving gadgets and fun-providing doodads. Such advertising is still very much with us, because it goes straight to the Silent Side and works directly on a powerful motive.

THE EXPECTATION MOTIVE

The Expectation Motive orients the nonconscious to the future. And the orientation is basically positive. No matter how pessimistic a person appears to be, expectation works within. Hope, trust and conviction that things will change for the better drives this motive.

Hope, trust and conviction prompt everyone to take risks necessary to change existing circumstances. Unless such risks are taken, life's challenge would cease to be of interest.

Every week, business calls take me through the town of Tunica, in the Mississippi Delta. Signs of rural poverty are everywhere. Yet, interestingly enough, about ten casinos have opened in the area within the last two years. And they're flourishing. Who are the high rollers keeping those casinos in business? They are local people, many of whom live on federal assistance. At the casinos, business picks up dramatically at the end of each month when welfare and Social Security checks arrive in the mail.

Lately, I noticed a huge number of used cars for sale in Tunica—too many. Because of my research into gambling motives, I wondered if the for-sale signs were the unhappy result of losing streaks at the casinos. Not so, I was told. People were selling their cars before they visited the casinos, piling up enough cash to stay in the game and win big.

I was floored. In Tunica, a 1970s vintage car is usually the only item many people can call their own. Yet, so strong was their expectation of impending wealth, dozens were ready to cash in their cars for a gambler's stake. Against all reason, and contrary to loud side logic, people were eager to take the plunge. For me, there is no starker example of the Expectation Motive's power than those cars for sale by the roadside in Tunica, Mississippi.

Another extreme but better publicized example of the Expectation Motive is the so-called "Cinderella Syndrome," in which women harbor a nonconscious belief that a handsome, virile and sensitive man will come galloping into their lives, rescuing them from depression, boredom and insensitivity. This syndrome is real. It may also be the underlying reason that the formulized literary genre of "women's romances" is so successful. Unrealistic? Of course. But the Expectation Motive is also undeniable.

Fulton observed a masculine counterpart to the Cinderella Syndrome in many factory workers he had supervised. He called his discovery the "99/1–1/99 Reversal Theory," a fancy name for a condition where ninety-nine out of one hundred workers practiced poor work habits because they nonconsciously believed that someday they would inherit money, be "discovered," hit the lottery, or whatever. Such expectations prevented them from knuckling down to a humdrum job they presumed was temporary. Although these workers thought they were shoo-ins for good fortune, Fulton estimated their chances at about one hundred to one, hence the name of his theory: "reversal."

The Expectation Motive comes into play when consumers need professional services. People often have no idea what is involved in placing their lives in the hands of a physician, psychiatrist or attorney. In each case, certain results are anticipated. If they do not materialize, the client learns to live with the outcome. In such settings, however, people seek more than results. They seek trust, confidence and optimism, all of which are components of the Expectation Motive. Because of the power of the Expectation Motive, and the inevitable naiveté of most consumers seeking professional services, almost all professional associations have licensing laws for the protection of clients.

Are the expectations of consumers reasonable? Often they are not, if they are measured by left-brain, loud side standards. Great care must be taken in marketing products where luck or arcane expertise plays a role. Doctors, lawyers, and casino operators, please take note.

THE PLAY MOTIVE

The decade of the 1990s has been called the Decade of the Brain. During that time we learned a lot about that mysterious organ between our ears.

One of the things that was turned up by researchers was the interesting motive of play. Everyone has seen a litter of puppies or kittens that within a few days begin to play with one another. This kind of play seems to have no particular purpose. It is not learned or conditioned, it just happens! Researchers have never really figured out the purpose of play, unless it is an inborn motive (like adaptation) designed to alleviate the problem of crowding in the nest. And that makes good sense.

Figure 3.1
The Structure of Human Motivation

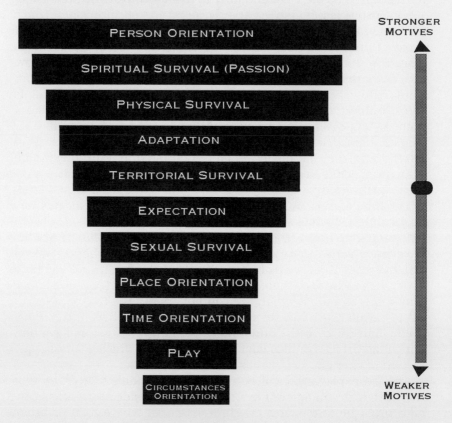

Although we recognize play as a motive, we have not investigated it. It is included here because it belongs, and further investigations are planned in the future. Play is usually seen in children seven years old and younger. At seven, a different motive becomes involved in play—the Territorial Motive—where the object is not only to play, but to win! Beyond that level, adult play will sometimes advance to the spiritual level, where the object is not only to win but to conquer, defeat and destroy!

THE HIERARCHY OF HUMAN MOTIVES

While reading this introduction to Silent Side motivations, you've probably noticed that some are much stronger, more robust motives than others. Figure 3.1 ranks nonconscious motivators in their order of importance, with the strongest at the top and the weakest at the base.

It is worth noting again that this ranking, although based on years of investigation, does not conform to traditional conclusions about human priorities. It also may not conform to logic or wishful thinking. The most important revelation was that avoiding spiritual death is one of the first and foremost motivators, even taking precedence over the prenatal Adaptation Motive. Spiritual survival is more powerful than physical survival, which has always been presumed dominant.

What about money? Our qualitative and quantitative research confirms that money is not and never has been a primary motivator. This conclusion will undoubtedly upset many behavioral psychologists who claim that money is a reinforcer, and that reinforcers are motivators. The Silent Side does not see things that way. The nonconscious is concerned with causes and reasons for human behavior, not the tactical pursuit of enablers. Money is simply a means for us all to get what we really want.

If your Adaptation Motive tells you it's important to own a Lexus to keep up with the neighbors, then you will need money to keep the Adaptation Motive from becoming frustrated. If your Personal Orientation Motive tells you it's important to change your looks, and your Expectation Motive tells you to trust good old Dr. Wintercorn not to ravage your face, money will get you the plastic surgery you crave. In every case, the Silent Side process is that you make a nonconscious decision about what you want; then you find a way to get it.

In management, money is a factor, not a motivator. To the manager, matters of money, greed, positioning, praise and status are valid considerations. But they are of secondary, not primary, importance. To find the motives for such secondary factors, a manager must look into the nonconscious mind.

Table 3.3 relates Silent Side motivations to the resulting whys and wherefores of consumer behavior. For the manager, this information is essential. For the leader, it's critical.

LEADERS ARE MOTIVATORS

The Silent Side operates simply. The four motivational groups summarized in this chapter are keys to successful leadership, for they explain why people do what you can predict them to do in the future (see Table 3.4). In upcoming chapters, we provide actual illustrations of Silent Side leadership in action, from the ground up.

Once you are familiar with Silent Side motivation, the value of this understanding becomes obvious. It provides a framework or a paradigm, which are not provided by other approaches to leadership.

Table 3.3
Motives, Elements, Emotions and Benefits in Human Behavior

MOTIVES	ELEMENTS	EMOTIONS	BENEFITS
Person Orientation	Self-control	Self-esteem Self-confidence Self-image	Renewal Acceptance Well-being
Place Orientation	Where	Escape Involvement Simplicity	Solutions Perspective Renewal
Time Orientation	When	Escape Involvement Simplicity	Relief Nostalgia
Circumstances Orientation	Convenience Pace (of life)	Relief from pressure Change Renewal Affirmation	Stability Regain perspective Forget hassles Relief
Spiritual Survival	Family values, Inner peace, Lawful order, Wholeness, Belonging, Witness significance, Affirming acceptance, Calling, Membership, Release, World-view, Human love, Sacrifice, Meaningful death	Love Passion Guilt Acceptance Dedication Perfection	Perfection Achievement Uniqueness Long life Endlessness Freedom from pain
Physical Survival	Food Air Water Shelter Excercise	Health and wellness Security Safety (from bodily harm)	Security Protection Safety Strength
Territorial Survival	Assets Career Income Competition Performance	Security	Achievement Power Status Control
Sexual Survival	Gender (M/F) Impulse (sex drive) Inhibition (female) Impotence (male)	Masculinity/Femininity Sexual satisfaction Control Security	Reproduction Enjoyment Self-expression Pleasure and play

Table 3.3 (*cont.*)
Motives, Elements, Emotions and Benefits in Human Behavior

MOTIVES	ELEMENTS		EMOTIONS	BENEFITS
Adaptation	Imitation		Security	Status
Motive	Learning		Confidence	Belonging
	Testimonials		Self-	Achievement
			assurance	Acceptance
			Low risk	
Expectation	Future		Trust	Commitment
Motive	Resolution		Hope	Confidence
			Faith	Decision
			Belief	making
Play Motive	Winning		Fun	Relief
	Excercise		Enjoyment	Resolution
			Creativity	Escape

Table 3.4
Motives and Their References

MOTIVES	REFERENCES
Person Orientation	Psychiatric Mental Status
Place Orientation	Examination: Goodman (1967)
Time Orientation	Friedman (1972), Seltzer (1994)
Circumstances Orientation	MacLean (1990)
Spiritual Survival	Fleischman (1990)
	Maddock and Fulton (1996)
	MacLean (1990)
Physical Survival	Maslow (1970)
Territorial Survival	Morris (1967)
Sexual Survival	We have no references for sexual survival. If you have any doubt as to the importance of this motive, then we suggest you consult your physician.
Adaptation Motive	Piaget (1971)
	Packard (1957)
Expectation Motive	Human: Kelly (1955), Vroom (1964), Rosenthal (1966)
	Animal: Hull (1943), Tolman (1932)
	Social Psychology: Festinger (1957), Lewin (1951)

It explains, and does not just describe what is taking place. It will become the most powerful predictor of success in leadership, and as seen in chapter 2, the motivational structure can be used repeatedly to structure an effective leadership program that will yield results every time.

REFERENCES

Festinger, L. (1957). *A theory of cognitive dissonance.* Evanston, IL: Row, Peterson.

Fleischman, P. (1990). *The healing spirit: Explorations into religion and psychiatry.* New York: Paragon House.

Friedman, A. M. (1972). *Diagnosing mental illness: Evaluation in psychology and psychiatry.* New York: Atheneum.

Goodman, J. (1967). *The child's mental status examination.* New York: Basic Books.

Hull, C. L. (1943). *Principles of behavior.* New York: Appleton-Century-Crofts.

Kelly, G. A. (1955). *The psychology of personal constructs.* New York: Norton.

Lewin, K. (1951). *Field theory and social science.* New York: Harper.

MacLean, P. D. (1990). *The triune brain in evolution: Role in paleocerebral functions.* New York: Plenum Press.

Maddock, R. C., & Fulton, R. L. (1996). *Marketing to the mind: Right brain strategies for advertising and marketing.* Westport, CT: Quorum Books.

Maslow, A. H. (1970). *Motivation and personality* (2nd ed.). New York: Harper & Row.

Morris, D. (1967). *The naked ape: A zoologist's study of the human animal.* New York: McGraw Hill.

Packard, V. O. (1957). *The hidden persuaders.* New York: D. McKay.

Piaget, J. (1971). *Mental imagery in the child: A study of the development of imaginal representation.* New York: Basic Books.

Rosenthal, R. (1966). Teacher's expectancies: Determinants of pupils' IQ gains. *Psychological Reports* 19, 115–118.

Seltzer, B. (1994). Psychiatric symptoms in Alzheimer's disease: Mental status examination vs. caregiver's report. *Gerontologist.*

Tolman, E. C. (1932). *Purposive behavior in animals and men.* New York: Appleton-Century-Crofts.

Vroom, V. H. (1964). *Work and motivation.* New York: Wiley.

Chapter 4

Integrating Motives and Emotions Into a Wholistic Pattern of Leadership

THE NEW ESSENTIALS OF LEADERSHIP

The theory of leadership presented in this book has the following implications:

- Leaders are made, and not born.
- Leadership involves the constructive use of emotion, which is already prevalent in organizations and in businesses but is suppressed, disguised and camouflaged.
- Effective leadership introduces nothing new or unique, but makes use of motives, emotions, features and benefits that are already in place.
- Motivation, for the first time, is defined.

If leadership is motivation and leaders are motivators, then it stands to reason that leaders are made, and not born. The missing link has been motivation. Therefore, all that is really necessary is to pick individuals who are, for one reason or another (seniority, technical expertise, friendliness, etc.), destined to become leaders in the organization and teach them about the structure and technology of human motivation. That structure was introduced in chapter 3, and is clarified and expanded in this chapter so that the organizational implications are clear and the applications are easier.

Bass (1997) did not deal directly with the role of emotion in leadership, or with motivation. However, he made the following statement:

> Socially oriented transformational leaders engage in the moral uplift-
> ing of their followers. Moral absolutes may be involved. It is absolutely
> true that crying "fire!" in a crowded theater is absolutely wrong. It is
> absolutely good to help the many without harming any. (p. 131)

In this statement, Bass spoke directly to the role of the Spiritual
Survival Motive because spiritual survival goes directly to the heart
of right versus wrong and good versus evil. But spiritual survival,
as indicated in chapter 3, is often confused with religion. When it
is, it is quickly dismissed by many as a motivator or an emotion, if
for no other reason except that religion is considered to be too controversial and also unscientific. Even Ashworth (1995), who called
for honesty in dealing with emotions in organizations, would stop
short of bringing religion, values and theology into the workplace.

However, some clarification may be needed here. In chapter 3, we
said that spiritual survival is not religion, per se, but it is whatever
people are passionate about. Furthermore, it was reported that psychologists, including Maslow, have actually missed the boat in not
dealing with what it is about which people are really passionate.
One reason for this is that psychologists like Maslow want to avoid
religion, because religion, as we know it, is not compatible with science and the scientific method. If that is the reason for excluding
religion, then it is a good one. But if that is the reason for excluding
passion, then it is at the very least a self-serving reason; that is, one
that serves the profession but not the people who are looking to the
profession for help and direction in their lives. It should also be
noted that a number of dictionaries and thesauruses use the word
"passion" to define religion.

Chidester (1996) added some clarification to this dilemma when
he went one step further by referencing an interview with Buck
O'Neill, "the great first baseman of the Kansas City Monarchs in the
1930's, who served baseball for over six decades as player, coach,
manager and scout." In the interview for a television series on the
history of baseball, O'Neill answered the question "What has a lifetime of baseball taught you?" Chidester quoted O'Neill as saying:
"Baseball is a religion. For me. You understand?" (p. 743).

O'Neill, in this interview, went on to say:

> Baseball is a religion because it is an enduring institution that is gov-
> erned by established rules. If you go by the rules, it is right. Baseball
> is a religion because it taught me and teaches everyone else to live by
> the rules and to abide by the rules. (p. 743)

Chidester stated four criteria that are satisfied and that establish
baseball as a church. Some of these criteria are comparable to

Fleischman's (1990) list of ten elements in religion, which will also turn out to be essential in building a model of effective leadership that is based on motivation and emotion.

First, Chidester said that baseball is a religion "because it insures a sense of continuity in the midst of a constantly changing America through the forces of tradition, heritage and collective memory" (p. 745). This is comparable to Fleischman's element of *lawful order*.

Second, baseball supports a sense of uniformity and a sense of belonging to something that is vast, and creates a microcosm within the real world. This is comparable to two of Fleischman's elements: *wholeness* and *membership*.

Third, baseball has a sanctuary, or a place of safety that is represented by home plate.

Fourth, the religion of baseball represents the sacred time of ritual.

Chidester then quoted Boswell (1994) who paraphrased Annie Savoy in the film, *Bull Durham*. In the opening speech, she makes a passionate statement about her devotion to baseball. "I believe in baseball," she declares, and then talks about how she has tried them all (Christianity, Buddha, Allah, trees, etc.) but "the only church that really feeds my soul is the church of baseball." Describing some of the external similarities between baseball and most of the more established Christian churches, she observes that both have rituals; both use organs and encourage the audience to join in the singing; the key players wear uniforms (vestments); they engage in superstitious practices that are designed to control outcomes, such as never stepping on the foul line, always spitting before entering the batter's box, carrying amulets and other good luck pieces, and so on. In fact, she even makes the observation of the "curious equivalence between 108 beads on the rosary and 108 stitches on a baseball."

From our own perspective of leadership and the new essentials, emotion is essential. And emotion is often seen in terms of right and wrong, good and evil, and in terms of who keeps the rules and who breaks them. This is passion, and this is what evokes emotion.

We believe also in the church of baseball, and even more so in football and basketball. The example given in chapter 3 of people leaving their homes under water in 1997 to go to the SEC playoffs adds even more support that professional sports have already obtained the status of a religion; not officially, but for many people who are "believers." We believe that just as the invention of the printing press was followed by a proliferation of churches all across Europe and Great Britain, the advent of television has seen, and will continue to see, more and more devotees falling into line as they follow favorite teams whom they have never even seen before in real life, but to whom they have absolute "do-or-die" loyalty, fidelity and devotion. Witness, for example, the ever increasing size of the "Subway Alumni" who follow Notre Dame religiously and passionately, but have never seen the team actually play in person, and who have no contact with Notre Dame outside of football. What would the average seven- or eight-year-old child, whose parents are members of the Subway Alumni, say when asked the question, "Is Notre Dame a university, or is it a football team?" Try it.

There is even some suspicion that the "science" of professional psychology is in fact a religion, and not a science. In a reply to a controversial article by Brown (1997, April) in the *American Psychologist*, Dineen (1998) states:

> In recent years, a shift has been occurring in which psychology is coming to be seen less and less as a science and to be presented as a religion replete with dogma and liturgical hierarchy. The principles of objectivity, rationality, reliability and validity are being replaced with the values of subjectivity, emotionality, peer consensus and client satisfaction.

THE INTEGRATION OF PASSION AND MOTIVATION INTO A COHERENT APPROACH TO LEADERSHIP

It is only a single step from the chaos of many different religions into a coherent explanation of leadership that completes the initial observation that Bass and others have started with respect to a coherent theory of leadership. This order starts with the elements described and defined by Fleischman (1990). It ends up in a logical and lucid formulary of leadership.

An example of this integration of leadership and the elements of religion is seen in Marine Corps recruit training, either at Parris Island, South Carolina or at MCRD San Diego (see Table 4.1). This was mentioned briefly in chapter 3. For years, the Marine Corps has been able to take self-centered, egocentric and totally narcissistic young men and fabricate leaders in just six to nine weeks. This is raw material that no one else could work with, even though they tried. No one else (school administrators, teachers, police, etc.) has even approached this accomplishment with groups of recalcitrant and delinquent young men. These were young men who were so demotivated that they even dropped out of high school, and then were retrained in the Marines and, in only six to nine weeks, they were ready to die for their country. The dynamics of this approach to leadership can only be understood in terms of Fleischman's ele-

Table 4.1
Motives Involved in USMC Basic Training

BASIC TRAINING SEQUENCE: U.S. MARINE CORPS
ACTIVITIES AND MOTIVATIONAL COMPONENTS

Action	*Motive/Element*
Destroy and undermine individuality and (reverse) individual self-confidence (Personal Orientation) with haircuts, uniforms, insults, regimens, etc.	Personal Orientation
Establish identity in USMC Uniforms, drills, lectures, physical training Establish training and set goals of training	Membership Affirmation and Acceptance (right and wrong) Sense of calling Lawful order
Establish readiness to defend, protect and lose life for one's country, if necessary	Sacrifice Meaningful death Sense of calling
Establish love for USMC, USA, freedom Training, playing patriotic songs, marching, parades, etc.	Human love Inner peace

---

ments of spiritual survival and the motives that are being introduced in this book. For example, in six to nine weeks the Marines typically accomplish what no one else could. But this is not by accident, it is by design. Although well known for their rigorous physical training and for getting recruits into shape, any drill sergeant truthfully admits that it's "95 percent psychological."

Some would object that this example is not a good one, for the Marines have a captive audience. They use authoritarian, militaristic methods, and they do things that could not be done in most organizations. Part of these objections may be acceptable, but the fact is, they still do it when no one else has been able to carry it off. Also, the Marines have been able to instill, in many cases, a lifetime of loyalty, devotion and allegiance that transcends what other service organizations have done. As Bass (1997) noted,

Transformational leadership may be autocratic and directive or it may be democratic and participative. Leaders can be intellectually stimulating to their followers when they authoritatively direct their followers' attention to a hidden assumption in their thinking. Leaders could also be intellectually stimulating when they ask whether their group would be ready to look together for hidden assumptions. (p. 136)

In other words, transformational leadership packages are not wrapped in the traditional red and green paper, but come in all colors and sizes. However, Bass may have erred when he spoke of leaders being intellectually stimulating. Our own findings strongly suggest that stimulation that is tied to the eleven motives introduced in chapter 3 is almost always emotional, not rational.

The importance of the elements that define spiritual survival and that have been elaborated by Fleischman (1990) is that they (a) are universal; (b) explain the underlying dynamics of all human need and human motivation within the Spiritual Survival Motive; (c) help to operationally define spiritual survival as a motive so that its meaning is not seen in the myriads of definitions of individual "churches"; and (d) explain why transformational and other forms of leadership work, just as they explain why Michelin sells more tires, why McDonald's sells more hamburgers and why Serta sells more mattresses.

As Seligman (1990) reminded us, behaviorists found they could not explain human behavior with animal behavior, except under very limited circumstances. This is because animals do not have an innate or inborn need for inner peace, love renewal or release. Furthermore, they do not have a sense of calling to their vocation, whether it involves catching mice or chasing down zebras. Finally, from what we can determine, animals have no thoughts about meaningful death. These elements, defined by Fleischman, not only clear up the whole issue of spirituality but also define what is unique in human behavior and what separates the human mind from the animal mind. They are also essential in terms of understanding what really motivates people and in the end, how to lead them.

SPIRITUAL SURVIVAL AS A VITAL ELEMENT IN LEADERSHIP

In a paper that won the 1993 Award for Distinguished Professional Contribution to Consumer Psychology, Krugman (1994) suggested that none of the core subdisciplines of psychology (industrial, organizational, clinical, etc.) have studied the likes and dislikes of people in general. He added that the everyday data of consumer research is the perfect forum for such a focus, presumably because the consumer psychologist is studying people where they spend their money. The unspoken implication of Krugman's work is that U.S. psychology in general and consumer psychology in particular have taken a self-limited approach to the study of human behavior. Much of it relied on Pavlov's research, which assumes that all behavior can be conditioned. Krugman concluded that "consequently, their research has investigated every other stimuli except the stimulus directly related to the response being studied" (p. 69).

We feel fortunate in that much of our own research has focused on consumers who are spending their money and their free time where they want to spend it, doing what they want to be doing and where they want to be doing it. If a person buys a $200,000 yacht and only visits it once or twice a year, he or she does it because being on the water gives the individual *peace of mind*. People whom we visited at boat shows have said they are satisfied by "just the fact that it is there and it's mine, and I can daydream about being on it, and end up with peace of mind." In other words, owning the boat is a $200,000 fantasy!

If a lot of people complain about Clinton's morality (or lack of morality), but still vote for him, it is because "Bill Clinton understands me, and my situation, and he knows what I'm going through." In Fleischman's (1990) terms, this is *witness significance*. It refers to the fact that there is "someone outside of myself in a position of power who understands me, and knows what I go through, each day, day after day. He's just like one of us!"

When a man who has already accumulated a small fortune continues to work day and night, six and seven days a week, it is obviously not the money that motivates him. Instead, it is what Fleischman referred to as *a sense of calling*. When a fireman risks his life and runs into a burning house to save a child or a pet, it's because of the need for sacrifice.

If people continue to eat fatty and high-cholesterol foods in spite of the dangers of heart disease, and then justify it on the basis of "my grandfather ate grease every day of his life, and lived until he was 92," their justification is based on a belief in fatalism and lawful order. We were told, in a study on nonfat foods, that many respondents believed "when your number is up, your number is up!" This was justified either on the basis of theology ("God has your number") or genetics. Most everyone is familiar with this philosophy, which is also referred to as *fatalism*.

These ten elements defined by Fleischman, along with family values, are critical in defining what people really want, and how they go about getting it. Look at any one of the behaviors just cited, and you might say "that's crazy! It's crazy to pay $200,000 for something you can't even enjoy! It's crazy to smoke or to load up on cholesterol and fat when a person has a family history of heart disease! It's crazy!" This is the way people have typically dealt with these behaviors: by writing them off as crazy or irrational, simply because we just could not understand them. But just like any other behavior—animal or human—they are the result of some causal factor or factors. Fleischman (1990), through his extensive cross-cultural and universal research, reported the bottom-line reasons for many of these behaviors or elements within the motive of spiritual survival. These elements have been applied to various aspects of consumer behavior, and they hold up in all cases. The result is a coherent approach to motivation that, unlike Maslow's (1970) approach, explains all human behavior, and not just facets of it.

What are the implications for leadership and leadership theory?

One implication is that leaders can be made, which means that we don't have to wait for them to be born. We are in no position to argue with Rose (1995) who, through twin studies, found that 40 percent of the variance in leadership qualities, as measured by the MLQ, are due to heritability factors. However, if leadership is motivation, then a person who knows how to motivate can be a leader because he or she can be trained in leadership by learning what motivation is and how it works. The problem previously has been that no one has adequately defined motivation. However, the motives, elements and factors that have been discussed here do define motivation, and all that is left is for individuals to learn how to put these principles into action. Individuals who do this will emerge as leaders, leaders who generate performance that is above and beyond all expectation and prediction!

BEYOND SPIRITUAL SURVIVAL

This chapter has dealt only with spiritual survival, which is one of the more powerful aspects of emotionality. In the factor analysis conducted on these motives and described in chapter 5, spiritual survival accounted for 9.2 percent of the variance. This was second only to the Personal Orientation Motive, which accounted for 13 percent. The Personal Orientation Motive is discussed in chapter 7.

Bass' (1997) Factor 1 is labeled *idealized influence*, which he called *charisma*. This factor is close to our Spiritual Survival Motive. His Factor 1 involves a number of affective components: trust, conviction, commitment and the ethical consequences of decisions. Other positive emotions include pride, loyalty, confidence and alignment around a shared purpose.

Bass' Factor 2, *inspirational motivation*, involves leaders who paint an attractive picture of the future and challenge followers with very high standards as well as new ways of doing things. This follows very closely and is most similar to our Expectation Motive. The Expectation Motive deals with an overall picture of the future, what it will be like and whether or not we will be prepared to handle it when it comes. Bass' inspirational motivation is similar because it deals with optimistic outlooks, encouragement and things that need to be done to ensure that everything turns out the way we want it to be, or at least close to it.

Bass' Factor 3, *intellectual stimulation*, does not appear to have a correlate in our system. We believe that this is because the system we have developed does not deal with intellectual and logical perspectives, but rather with emotions and motives.

Bass' Factor 4, *individualized consideration*, appears to be close to our Personal Orientation Motive. In individualized consideration, leaders deal with people as individuals; listen, advise, teach and coach them and take into consideration the special needs that each person has and how they contribute to the overall picture.

The factors that Bass has uncovered and the ones that are listed here are not oppositional to each other. Instead, they are complementary because Bass is not talking about nonconscious motivation, and that is all we are covering here. When our research was originally conducted with consumers, we purposely ignored the rational motives, such as price, value, cost and so on. The results were encouraging, for they allowed us to deal with a whole new frontier in psychological research—the frontier of verbal and nonverbal nonconscious motives.

SO WHY DO WE CHOOSE SO MANY IMPAIRED LEADERS?

Hogan, Curphy and Hogan (1994), in their review of the traits involved in leadership selection and success, questioned why individuals choose impaired leaders. Their review heavily emphasizes leadership *traits*. It should first be pointed out that our approach to leadership is not a trait theory. The problem with trait-based approaches to leadership is that they are descriptive, not explanatory. We believe, as stated previously, that leaders can be made. Our belief springs from the whole idea that leadership is motivation, and therefore if an individual knows what motivation is, he or she knows how to lead. In the past, the failure has been the inability to define what motivates people, and to specify what makes people do what it is they do.

Hogan et al. referenced a 50 percent failure among senior executives, which they said is due to the use of flawed selection methods. These authors were adamant that many leaders are chosen using invalid methodologies, or in some cases, no methodologies at all.

Another reason they believed managers and executives fail is because of what they called *dark-side* characteristics. According to the statistics they gathered, managers with so-called dark-side characteristics can, through training, reverse many of these characteristics and traits, but Hogan et al. questioned whether this training has any lasting results.

From the perspective presented here, the comprehensive motivational approach can address all of the problems in human behavior, and in many cases can provide a solution for them because they focus on the causes of behavior, rather than just the results. This is an extremely important difference. The success of the "medical model" during the last half of this century has taught that solutions come through dealing with the causes of disease, and not just with the symptoms. The findings here are similar when it comes to dealing with behavior, and not with the symptoms or outcomes.

WHY LEADERS FAIL

The cause of failure in any area of human or interpersonal relations is brought about by shifting or transposing the levels within the pyramid. The pyramid, which appears in Figure 3.1, has eleven levels. Generally the levels appear as they are shown in the model. Occasionally, they get rearranged. Rearrangement for any length of time can cause major problems.

For example: A computer operator spends considerably more hours at work than he is being paid for, partially because he is having problems at home but also because he enjoys his work. He becomes more and more committed to his work, and within a few months it becomes a spiritual commitment rather than a territorial one. In other words, he shifts his motivation to put in long hours from territorial survival to spiritual survival, and begins to rationalize it with spiritual arguments. With this spiritual commitment to his work, he begins to spend even more time and effort than he did before. Nonconsciously, however, he begins to resent the fact that no one notices his extra effort, and no one seems to care. This realization can then lead to a number of impaired behaviors: stealing from the company to get "what's rightfully mine"; badmouthing senior executives, management and stockholders; sabotaging the work efforts of others and taking time off during the day when he is supposed to be available. All of this is because of the nonconscious feeling that he has been cheated out of what is rightfully his.

Another example involves the confusion between the Territorial Survival Motive and the Sexual Survival Motive, which is a common occurrence in many organizations. For example: The manager in a proof transit operation in a bank has a number of young females working for him, and begins to view them as "my harem" or a "stall." This is because of the personal power that he holds over them and their lifestyles. Territorial power and sexual power are easily confused because these motives are very close to each other in the pyramid. The manager becomes increasingly demanding of personal favors, eventually threatening termination or failure to promote unless sexual favors are granted. This is a somewhat extreme but also common and ordinary situation, and is another example of how serious problems arise within an organization when levels are shifted in the motivational pyramid. Territorial interests give way to sexual priorities. The solution, as in all these cases, can only be a reordering or reshifting of the priorities. Anything else would be "symptom relief" and as such would be superficial and have very little effect.

It should be apparent that a large number of problems are related to the shifting of priorities. Companies have policies about fraternization between employees, and it is generally known that fraternization leads to larger problems. However, it is not known exactly why this occurs. The problem—and this is true in almost all issues, at work and at home—is that priorities get inadvertently shifted in the pyramid of human motivation.

Another simpler and more straightforward example of the shifting of priorities on the pyramid is when a person elects to drink or smoke heavily. This decision involves a "trade-off" between the Adaptation Motive ("Everyone else is doing it") and the Physical Survival Motive ("It's not good for me!"). See how the motives and priorities get shifted around?

LEADERSHIP: A SURREALISTIC WORLD

Long before Watergate, it was very apparent that leaders have flaws, and that leaders are human. Watergate signaled the entry into the age of electronic recording devices that were small enough to be effectively hidden so that people could "snoop." As we left the Watergate era of the 1970s and entered the '80s and '90s, the use of electronic surveillance devices including wire taps, hidden video cameras and other reconnaissance methods, became more common. As they did, more leaders were caught in the mousetrap. Leaders are now seen on a much larger scale for what they really are: ordinary people, "just like you and me."

The 1990s brought a flurry of discoveries. Such notables included Dan Rostenkowski, Mel Reynolds, President Clinton and a number of his appointees—those involved in various Senate and House banking scandals, and also in sexual frays. Initially it is shocking, but then quickly becomes conventional and undistinguished, as it increasingly appears as if "everyone is doing it." Then it becomes fodder for the talk show hosts and eventually, sooner or later, these characters fade into obscurity.

Leadership carries with it some privileges and perks that make it desirable, seductive and alluring. But it also brings with it some dangers.

The world of leadership is a world of surrealism. What distinguishes a surrealistic world from a "real" world is the lack of boundaries. Look at a surrealistic painting, and you will see that what distinguishes it from other art is that the boundaries or borders are fuzzy, ambiguous and misty. They blend together. This is the characteristic that seduces the person who enters this special world of leadership. It is the ambiguity to stretch or even redefine the boundaries, and to make new interpretations. Because the borders and boundaries are vague, there is room for review, reinterpretation and reinvention. Much of what can and can't be done is left up to individual judgment, which varies widely and is often dependent on background, breeding and past development.

An example of this is when Coach Barry Switzer of the Dallas Cowboys attempted to walk through an airport security gate with a loaded pistol. No ordinary citizen can do that, and he discovered he couldn't do it either. But Switzer is the coach of an NFL team that is not just a regional team, like the Green Bay Packers or the Philadelphia Eagles. The Cowboys are "America's Team" (according to their home page). Anyone who coaches the Cowboys—or anyone who plays for them—is in a special, rarefied atmosphere. They are set aside. They have special rules that govern them. And these rules are very elastic. This may also explain why more of their players have had personal problems than the players on other more controlled teams.

During the time of the House banking scandal, it never occurred to a number of representatives that what they were doing—writing checks without money to cover the checks—was illegal. They knew the rules, but at the same time they operated in a different environment. They were in a surrealistic environment where the boundaries were not clearly defined.

This exception from ordinary rules—this surrealism—is typical whenever an activity, such as football or baseball, becomes "spiritualized." People who are spiritual leaders, like well-known politicians, coaches and others associated with spiritual-level endeavors, also exempt themselves from the rules. This observation has no arguments, no disagreements. We have seen it repeatedly among "real" religious and spiritual leaders: Swaggart, Jones and the Bakkers; and among political leaders who are living in that same rare-fied atmosphere. They believe that because of their "spiritual" status, they are exempt from the rules.

It is possible that at no place or time in our history were surre-alism and complete loss of boundaries more apparent than in the Clinton-Lewinski affair. The boundaries were not just blurred in this situation, they were nonexistent. When Americans finally got beyond the voyeuristic and sensationalistic aspects of the Starr Report, it was clear that their President had taken enormous and incalculable risks, well beyond the boundaries of what anyone would expect of someone in a leadership position. When these risks were apparent to almost everyone, questions were immediately raised about his judgment and acumen, and subsequently about his ability to function as a world leader.

Not only did Bill Clinton feel that he was not accountable for his sexual activities but he apparently also felt that, in his position as President, he could also safely lie to his constituents and to all Americans. This was because in his role he did not feel constrained by the boundaries that apply to everyone else. And in spite of his obvious characterological flaws, the political polls which came out shortly after this affair was exposed still reflected considerable popular support. This popular support was based on his charisma as a leader and his ability to motivate, and not upon his character or moral turpitude.

We take exception with Hogan et al. (1994) and others who believe that better selection methods will lead to leaders who are more stable and less vulnerable. Anyone who is selected and who then enters that special surrealistic world is vulnerable. Leadership is not a constellation of traits. Leadership is motivation.

The first of the eleven major motives, spiritual survival, has been covered in this chapter. It is a powerful motive, but when it is understood and practiced within the eleven elements covered here, it can not only be controlled, but it can be used productively in the leadership design, selection and prediction of leaders and leadership programs. This is because we can now explain emotion and understand motivation, which is the goal of science. Others are limited to description and narration of what is happening in front of them. The Silent Side allows explanation, solution and revelation.

There is nothing new about defining leadership as motivation and leaders as motivators. But the key is in defining motivation, which is what the Silent Side is all about.

REFERENCES

Ashworth, B. E. (1995). Emotion in the workplace: A reappraisal. *Human Relations 48*(2), 97.

Bass, B. M. (1997). Does the transactional–transformational leadership paradigm transcend organizational and national boundaries? *American Psychologist 52*(2), 130–139.

Boswell, T. (1994). The church of baseball. In G. C. Ward & K. Burns (Eds.), *Baseball: An illustrated history*. New York: Alfred A. Knopf.

Brown, L. S. (1997). The private practice of subversion: Psychology as tik-kun olam. *American Psychologist 52*, 449–462.

Chidester, D. (1996). The church of baseball, the fetish of Coca-Cola and the potlatch of rock n' roll: Theoretical models for the study of religion in American popular culture. *Journal of the American Academy of Religion 64*(4), 743–764.

Dineen, T. (1998). Sacred cows and straw men. *American Psychologist 54*(4), 487–488.

Fleischman, P. (1990). *The healing spirit. Explorations in religion and psychotherapy*. New York: Paragon House.

Hogan, R., Curphy, G. J., & Hogan, J. (1994). What we know about leadership: Effectiveness and personality. *American Psychologist 49*(6), 493–504.

Krugman, H. E. (1994). Pavlov's dog and the future of consumer psychology. *Journal of Advertising Research 34*(6), 67–71.

Maslow, A. H. (1970). *Motivation and personality* (2nd ed.). New York: Harper & Row.

Rose, R. (1995). Genes and human behavior. *Annual Review of Psychology 46*, 625–654.

Seligman, M. E. P. (1990). *Learned helplessness*. New York: Pocket Books.

Chapter 5

The Origins of Motives and Emotions

THREE-POINT PROTOCOL

Typically when a theory is put forward in the literature it is subjected to empirical validation. In other words, a hypothesis is generated around the format that *if we do this . . . then this will happen.* Data is collected to see if there is any validity to the theory, and the hypothesis is tested. The ultimate test in most psychological research is statistical, and the statistical test that is applied to all research is the rejection of the null hypothesis at the .001, .01 or .05 level. What the researcher wants to say in the end analysis is that there are only five chances in one hundred (or 1, or .01) that the results of this experiment occurred by chance and chance alone. That instead, the results are due to the experimental manipulation, whatever that might be.

In looking at motivation, we have relied on validation from three sources. The first source is statistics in the form of factor analysis. This is an inferential method that is addressed in this chapter.

The second source of validation for this approach to leadership is advertising, which was presented in chapter 3. It is briefly reviewed in this chapter, not with the intention of repeating everything that was said in chapter 3, but merely to show why advertising can be used as a reliable and important source of validation.

The third source of validation is neurological substrates of motivation. During the late 1980s and early '90s, significant research was carried out on the brain and particularly on the brain's limbic system, which is the center of emotion and sensation. Out of this research have come the new neuroleptic medications, such as Pro-zac, Paxil, Xanax and others. Because of our newfound knowledge of the emotional centers of the brain, we are able to specifically ad-dress the origin of the motives that have been introduced in chapter 3, in terms of their neurological substrates. The relation between the various motives, their origin and their correlates in the anatomy of the brain is discussed in chapter 6.

WHERE DO MOTIVES COME FROM?

Before getting into two of the three areas of validation that are discussed in this chapter, it would be appropriate first to address the question "Where do motives come from in the first place?" This question is often asked in seminars and presentations, and it should be apparent that most of these motives have had their or-igin in the nonconscious mind. But specifically, the question we have addressed in seminars is "Where do the individual groups of motives come from? The Orientation Motives? The Survival Mo-tives? What is their origin?" That is the question addressed at this point.

THE ORIENTATION MOTIVES

The Orientation Motives are the basis and the foundation of the psychiatric mental status test, and have been for at least one hun-dred years (Taylor, 1988). Because of various conditions, alcohol, injuries, strokes, seizures and most notably from old age, when the "parts" begin to wear out from use, people may sometimes become disoriented. There are also other conditions where disorientation is a symptom. One of those conditions is psychosis, a condition related to several different kinds of mental illness and generally considered severe. In most states, McNaughton's rule applies, where a person who is being tried and found guilty of a crime can be, if found psy-chotic, given an alternative sentence. Such a sentence might be to a state hospital rather than to a state penitentiary. Such was the case with John Hinkley, who shot at Ronald Reagan during the be-ginning of his presidency. Under McNaughton's rule, psychosis is defined in terms of the ability to distinguish between right and wrong.

It has also been known for the last one hundred years that there are three types of orientations: to person, to place and to time. Some have added a fourth, which is orientation to circumstances ("Do you know why you are here today?"). In psychiatry, the mental status test is the cornerstone and the centerpiece of every psychiatric interview. It is always used to determine whether a person is competent enough to manage his or her own affairs, but it is not the only test of competency. It should be sufficient, however, to say that there are other tests of competency and then leave it at that because the only issue of importance in motivation is these mental states.

From experience, we know that these four mental states are not equal. This is because an individual who is aging will always lose orientation to circumstances first, then time, then place and finally to person. This is true in dreams, which also arise from the nonconscious. In a dream you may be in a place where you lived many years ago (orientation to place), with people who are now deceased and yet it seems to be taking place at the present time (orientation to time). However, you have probably noticed that in a dream, although the place, time and circumstances may change, you remain the same. In your dreams you are always the same person.

The mental status test and specifically the four orientation states have never been used to describe motivation, until now. In the research described in chapter 3, it became clearer to us that these four *states* were also motives. In English, what we did is convert nouns into verbs. This is referred to as the *verbalization of a noun*. Note that this is not an unusual or isolated procedure, but is seen all the time. An example would be when the word *party* is converted to *partying*.

In chapter 3, we made reference to the research we conducted in casinos. Casino gaming is one of the fastest growing "industries" in America. It is also well known by casino management that people don't go to casinos just to win money. There is another set of motives that is probably more important than winning, and that is the Orientation Motives. When entering a casino it should be apparent that management does everything it can to disorient the customer, because that's what the customer wants: There are no windows (disorientation to time); where state law allows, alcohol is provided (disorientation to circumstances); frequent visitors are treated like big shots (disorientation to person); and the gaming floor is usually dimly lit with loud and disorienting "music" that is not like any music heard anyplace else (disorientation to time [timing, beat] and disorientation to place).

Although it is imperative that we remain oriented when we are at work, or driving a car or exercising responsibility as a parent, it is tiring. And so we search out and look for disorienting experiences. The problem comes in when people impose these disorienting experiences on school, or the workplace or in other situations where orientation is crucial. This is the challenge of the Orientation Motives to leadership, and it is addressed in four separate chapters in this book.

THE SURVIVAL MOTIVES

Maslow (1970) made it clear that motivation is a matter of survival. However, we feel he overlooked three important aspects of survival: spiritual survival, sexual survival and territorial survival. Each of these important motives is discussed in chapters that follow: spiritual survival in chapter 8 and in several other places in the book, territorial survival in chapter 10 and sexual survival in chapter 11.

Spiritual survival could easily become a "wastebasket" category because it is so broad and nondescriptive. However, when explained in terms of Fleischman's (1990) elements of religion, it becomes operationally defined. These elements can be applied in areas outside of religion and theology in order to explain behavior that seems irrational or unexplainable. One area we have researched and that illustrates the application of these elements to irrational behavior is why people spend their life savings to visit Graceland, Elvis Presley's home, and why it is the second most visited house in America (Maddock & Fulton, 1996).

Territorial survival was well defined by Morris (1967) in a landmark book on that subject. Furthermore, there is substantial evidence in the animal kingdom of animals fighting to their death over territorial rights; another indication that physical survival is not the bottom line. Monkeys urinate around the perimeter of their territory, birds spread their wings and dogs bark. In the pages of prehistory and the dawn of man we read that the man defined the territory and the woman stayed behind and took care of it. We still see vestiges of our ancestors' activities when we look at the list of best-selling men's magazines (e.g., *Field & Stream* and *Motortrend*) versus women's magazines (*Better Homes and Gardens* and *Family Circle*). There are also innate characteristics seen in men and women that are most likely traced back to the dawn of history, such as men having a much better sense of direction than women, and women having a much better sense of intuition than men.

Interestingly, when we are asked about references on the Sexual Survival Motive we are hard pressed to find them. Where do we look, or who do we consult? At the same time, is there anyone who would doubt the motivational power of sex? Studies with animals have shown that when rats are placed in a Skinner box and given a choice between pressing a bar that delivers a very mild electrical charge to the medial forebrain bundle of the brain or pressing a bar for food, they will select the former, almost to the point of starvation (Olds & Milner, 1954). This procedure was referred to as *intercranial self-stimulation* (ICS) and it is believed that it brought the animal to the point of, but not including, ejaculation or an orgasm. Here again, the priority of the Physical Survival Motive is called into question.

In our opinion, the best place to look for references that document the power of the Sexual Survival Motive and the sex drive in motivation is in advertising. For years, sex has been used as a motivator, particularly in appeals made to men. Because boats or yachts almost always represent an impulse purchase decision, boats that appear in boat shows almost always feature a beautiful, well-built woman in a bikini, draped across the bow. This draws the man to the boat, which is 50 percent of the sales effort. The other 50 percent is in getting him to write the check. Similarly, sex has been used effectively to market women's impulse products, particularly fragrances and certain kinds of leisure attire and lingerie. More recently, it has been used to sell jeans and a wide variety of articles of clothing.

THE ADAPTATION MOTIVE

Like the Sexual Survival Motives, advertising is replete with testimonials and "me-tooisms" that reflect the power of the Adaptation Motive in the real world. Most people select a physician, dentist or attorney on the basis of someone else's recommendation because very few of us have the proper credentials to decide who is or is not a good doctor or surgeon. We often buy cars for the same reason, or make other major purchases. We want to live in a neighborhood where there are "people like us." We often buy products on the basis of a testimonial by a revered sports hero or movie star. In psychology, Piaget (1970) discussed the importance of both the Adaptation Motive and the Assimilation Motive in the growth process. And in nonverbal behavior (Maddock & Fulton, 1995), we have seen the priority of the Adaptation Motive even in utero, as the infant moves his or her hands up to the face and head in a primitive effort to adapt to that environment. Adaptation takes a different course in adolescence, as we begin to mimic and copy everything our peers are doing. It is now well conceded and agreed on that this is how smoking gets started because most people who start smoking will do so in early, middle or late adolescence.

THE EXPECTATION MOTIVE

The variable of expectation or expectancy has been used in a number of contexts and as a central or key issue in any discussion of motivation. It has its roots in human motivation (McClelland, Atkinson, Clark, & Lowell, 1953; Vroom, 1964), in animal learning (Hull, 1952 ; Tolman, 1932), developmental psychology (Ford, 1987; Piaget, 1970), social psychology (Feather, 1966; Klinger, 1977; Lewin, 1951; Rosenthal & Jacobsen, 1968), personality (Bandura 1977; Mischel, 1973), clinical psychology (Kelly, 1955; Norem & Cantor, 1986; Rotter, 1954; Scheier & Carver, 1992) and in other areas. It permeates the literature in psychology in all areas. It is, according to MacLean (1990), our adaptation to the future.

THE PLAY MOTIVE

The Play Motive was validated by MacLean when he stated that activities involving play are unique to mammals, along with nursing and audio-vocal communication between parent and offspring. He noted particularly that the purpose of play is not clear, and that it appears spontaneously without any particular outcome or consequence. He hypothesized that it may have had the original purpose of relieving the tension that results from crowding in the nest. In humans, play may be a form of conscious or "awake" dreaming, that is, working out the impact of the day's events on the psyche, by way of controlled diversion.

In our culture, play at that adult level is really not play. It is competitive, aggressive and very ambitious. In many cases play has become big business (NFL, NBA, NCAA, etc.) and undoubtedly (when combined with television) is one of the biggest businesses of our time. In our treatment of motives, most play is discussed in terms of either territorial survival (competition) or spiritual survival (do or die, fight-to-the-death survival). The exception is when dealing with the play of children, which is what this motive is all about. There are also a few adult activities, such as square dancing or going to a movie, that would be appropriately categorized as play because they have no stated purpose or outcome.

THE EMPIRICAL SIDE OF LEADERSHIP

The approach to motivation that has been presented in this book is exploratory and is based on informal and formal hypotheses about how the structure of the theory measures the constructs. Factor-analytic studies are an important way of verifying whether the underlying hypotheses are correct.

Two separate confirmatory factor-analytic studies were carried out in order to gain support for the motives and their elements that have been presented in chapter 3. The first involved a general life-style questionnaire that was given to a population of adults in evening and summer classes in two different community colleges. Also involved in this study were factory workers in a midwestern printing operation and another group, most of whom were employees of a community hospital.

The second confirmatory factor analysis looked exclusively at Fleischman's elements of religion because we have found, in all our studies with consumers, that consumer motivation and indeed all human motivation at the spiritual level can be understood and interpreted only with the assistance of these elements. Also, and as explained in chapters 4 and 7, without these elements the concept of spiritual survival becomes undefinable and at best, a wastebasket category for weird and far-out statements. For example, on the Rorschach Ink Blot examination, most responses that appear to be "spiritual" in nature are assigned to such a wastebasket category that is called *special scores* (Exner, 1993).

Initial Confirmatory Factor Analysis on Lifestyles

A confirmatory factor-analytic study was carried out with a life-style questionnaire. The questionnaire was designed around items that described the various motives in the hierarchy. Prior to this confirmatory factor analysis, several exploratory factor analyses were carried out in order to sort through the different variables (questions, or items). As in most preliminary or exploratory factor analyses, some questions are eliminated and some are retained. Two exploratory factor analyses were carried out on respondents from various settings, but most were enrolled in undergraduate classes at two colleges in eastern Arkansas. Although many of these were adults enrolled in courses that were taught in the evening division, in order to broaden the age range of the respondents in these exploratory studies, they were invited to bring their parents, friends or neighbors to a session in which they could fill out the questionnaires. After two of these exploratory factor analyses it was felt that there were a sufficient number of items that were predictive and not overlapping to conduct a confirmatory factor analysis.

Table 5.1
Results of First Lifestyle Questionnaire Factor Analysis

FACTOR #	FACTOR NAME	VARIANCE (% OF TOTAL)
1	Person Orientation	13.0
2	Spiritual Survival	9.2
3	Sexual Survival: Gender (Female)	5.9
4	Adaptation Motive	5.1
5	Sexual Survival: Impulse (Male)	4.5
6	Physical Survival	4.0
7	Expectation: Optimism	3.8
8	Place Orientation I	3.6
9	Circumstances Orientation	3.3
10	Expectation: Pessimism	2.9
11	Sexual Survival: Gender (Male)	2.7
12	Territorial Survival (Female)	2.7
13	Time Orientation	2.5
14	Place Orientation II	2.3
15	Sexual Survival: Impulse (Female)	2.1
16	Sexual Survival: Inhibition (Female)	2.0
17	Sexual Survival: Impulse (Male/Female)	1.9
18	Spiritual Survival II (Gun Ownership)	1.9

Confirmatory Factor Analysis on Eleven-Motive Hierarchy

Respondents in this project included students in two different university settings, factory workers in a midwestern printing operation and hospital employees. All were volunteers. The questions on the lifestyle questionnaire were derived from descriptions of day-to-day activities that were found in several exploratory factor analyses to describe and be related to the motives and their elements.

In this research a 125-item questionnaire was administered. The results of this first factor analysis and rotations are seen in Table 5.1.

There are only eleven motives in the pyramid (the Play Motive was not included in the hierarchy at the time that this research was carried out), whereas Table 5.1 lists eighteen. This is because the Sexual Survival Motive broke out into the three elements of sexual survival: gender, impulse and inhibition. This illustrates a point made in chapter 3, which is that sex cannot be addressed as an issue, but rather in terms of its three elements. For example, if a person has a sexual problem and presents to a physician for treatment, the first thing the physician has to know is whether it is an impulse problem, a gender problem or a problem with inhibition.

The Territorial Survival Motive also broke down into gender differences, as expected. The motives of men and women within the Territorial Survival Motive are much different. Very few women choose duck hunting as a recreational preference, and very few men enjoy shopping for new fabrics for decorating the home. There are, of course, always exceptions and there always will be.

Finally, the Expectation Motive broke down into differences between people with optimistic expectations and those with pessimistic expectations. This was not expected, but should have been. The Expectation Motive cannot be dealt with by focusing only on positive outcomes. Many years of psychological research have shown that if there is one solid, dependable and reliable finding in the area of personality research, it is that there are some people who are pessimistic and some who are optimistic, as well as those who are extroverted and those who are introverted.

Based on the outcome of this first confirmatory factor analysis, we have described 70 percent of the variance in motives and motivation.

Second Exploratory Factor Analysis on Fleischman's Ten Elements of Religion

A second factor analysis took place on Fleischman's (1990) elements of spiritual survival because they play such an important role in motivation in general and in spiritual survival specifically.

In our work with consumers, the importance of the Spiritual Survival Motive was obvious. Also it was clearly identified in the first factor analysis that was carried out. However, even though it was identified it was difficult to work with because it was hard to define. Eventually, we were able to define it in terms of passion; that is, whatever people tend to be passionate about. A man can be religious in the traditional sense, but his real passion may be golf, fishing, hunting, the NBA and so forth. The next step was to operationalize this motive, and this is where Fleischman's elements of spiritual survival were essential. For example, when an individual buys a mattress he or she has no interest in its construction because what the consumer is looking for is inner peace. Selection of a new refrigerator to replace an old one contains, surprisingly enough, a spiritual element because the first criterion is size, and size is based on servicing the family dinner that may only occur once or twice a year.

When people continue to eat foods that are harmful to their physical survival their behavior is partially motivated by fatalism and lawful order. This is because, at the nonconscious level, they believe that longevity in life is either controlled by genetics and inheritance or controlled by God. Hence, fatalism. Lawful order is an element of spiritual survival. As reported in chapter 1, when people vote, the primary consideration is whether the leader they are voting for understands them personally and what they have been through personally in their lives (witness significance). In the case of Clinton, "He's just like me, and he understands what I have to go through."

These things become obvious in the area of consumer psychology because advertising works and what people say is usually supported by what they buy. But it is not too obvious in other areas of psychology. Therefore, in the interest of gaining more empirical support for these elements and being able to operationalize spiritual survival as a motive, this second factor analysis was completed.

This methodology was essentially the same as the first two just described. Fleischman's book *The Healing Spirit* was used to define and word the questions or items. Fleischman was consulted for his input. There were ten questions for each one of the ten elements, for a total of one hundred questions or items. Respondents were undergraduates in psychology classes, health care personnel in a local hospital and graduate students in a course on statistics and research design in education. The protocol was in a five-point Likert-type format and one hundred sixty protocols were completed. The results are seen in Table 5.2.

The implications of this factor analysis and the support it provides for Fleischman's structure and to this whole approach to leadership are strong. The implications for transformational leadership are also significant.

The examples of successful leadership, such as the ones discussed in chapter 8 at Eastman or in chapter 3 in Marine Corps recruit training, can be replicated over and over again, by large or small organizations, by incorporating the most salient elements of Fleischman's hierarchy. Furthermore, leaders can be trained in the principles of motivation, thereby answering and responding directly to the old and ongoing dilemma, "Are leaders born, or are they made?"

Table 5.2
Results of Confirmatory Factor Analysis on Fleischman's Ten Elements of Religion

FACTOR #	FACTOR NAME	VARIANCE ACCOUNTED FOR (%)
1	Witness Significance	11.3
2	Membership	7.8
3	Renewal and Release	4.5
5	Sacrifice[a]	3.3
6	Lawful Order	3.1
8	Affirming Acceptance	2.6
9	Affirming Acceptance II	2.5
10	Renewal and Release II	2.4
11	Human Love	2.2
12	Calling	2.1
13	Inner Peace[b]	2.0
	Total Variance Accounted for (%)	43.8

[a]Factor 4, pace (of life), was the only factor that was not part of the ten elements of spiritual survival, but it accounted for 3.7 percent of the variance. This issue is addressed by Fleischman in his book and lectures.
[b]The one factor that was not accounted for in the first ten was meaningful death. Some of the variables that appeared to describe this variable were grouped with lawful order on Factor 6.

IMPLICATIONS AND IMPORTANCE OF THESE RESULTS

The bottom line of this approach to leadership is not intended to oversimplify this complex and long debated issue. It is intended, however, to bring something new to the table, and that is motivation. When leadership is redefined in terms of motivation, and motivation is seen in terms of the eleven motives that have been laid out and illustrated in this book, the whole concept of *leadership* takes a giant step toward objectivity and scientific status. The fact that it is not objective and not scientific is the reason that its ingredients and its structure are still being argued and cannot be agreed on.

In chapter 4, the work of Hogan, Curphy, and Hogan (1994) was reviewed and the emphasis was on the use of scientific psychometric strategies in order to choose more effective leaders. Also in chapter 4, the work of Bass (1997) on transformational leadership was covered and it was shown how transformational leadership, although not dealing directly with emotion, does incorporate what we refer to as *witness significance* and also *membership*, the two most influential elements in the hierarchy of spiritual survival. However, a problem is seen with both Hogan et al.'s and Bass' approaches in that they both rely on Maslow's (1970) hierarchy as a basis for motivation. This brings in the problems discussed in chapter 2: Maslow's theory is unscientific and has more of a status of a belief system than it does as a credible, scientific explanation that deals with fact. This problem, in turn, uncovers many other issues. For example, how can we use as a basis for our whole approach an unscientific, invalidated and unsubstantiated belief system and at the same time advocate a scientific approach? Isn't a chain as strong as its weakest link? Another problem that arises is how we can possibly select, promote, train, encourage or even recognize leaders when we cannot identify what motivates nonleaders, or "followers." In addition, the goal of science is replication. How can a leadership program be replicated if we don't know the basic ingredients of the most important parts of that program, and that is motivation?

In contrast, the approach presented here relies on the three-dimensional structure discussed in the introduction: advertising, our knowledge of neuroanatomy (chapter 6), and empirical support and validation (this chapter). As a result, this motivational approach, which is consistent and not "out of sync" with other scientific theories, such as Darwin's evolution of species, is capable of predicting, designing, replicating, duplicating, simulating, identifying and diagnosing leaders and leadership patterns whenever they occur and wherever they may be.

As it turns out, Fleischman in his original investigations did not intend for the ten elements to extend beyond the field of religion and religious studies, except insofar as they applied to a clinical, psychotherapeutic relationship. However, because our own investigations in advertising, marketing and leadership have gone well beyond this, we have found that these elements have widespread applications as well as implications in many fields of study. They can be used in explaining significant variance in human behavior in many different areas. Unfortunately, when psychologists left out or overlooked the area of religion, they "threw out the baby with the bath water." What they did not recognize when they did this was that there are many different varieties of religions and religious beliefs which, if defined in terms of these elements, can be understood as individual pursuits of spiritual survival, which now has the substantial empirical support and validation that has been presented in this chapter.

REFERENCES

Bandura, A. (1977). Self-efficacy. Toward a unifying theory of behavioral change. *Psychological Review 84*, 191–215.

Bass, B. M. (1997). Does the transactional-transformational leadership paradigm transcend organizational and national boundaries? *American Psychologist 52*(2), 130–139.

Exner, J. E. (1993). *The Rorschach technique: A comprehensive system* (3d ed., Vol. 1). New York: John Wiley and Sons.

Feather, N. T. (1966). Effects of prior success and failure on expectations of success and subsequent performance. *Journal of Personality and Social Psychology 3*, 287–298.

Fleischman, P. R. (1990). *The healing spirit.* New York: Paragon.

Ford, D. H. (1987). *Humans as self-constructing living systems: A developmental perspective on behavior and personality.* Hillsdale, NJ: Lawrence Erlbaum.

Hogan, R., Curphy, G. J., & Hogan, J. (1994). What we know about leadership: Effectiveness and personality. *American Psychologist 49*(6), 493–504.

Hull, C. L. (1952). *A behavior system: An introduction to behavior theory concerning the individual organism.* New Haven, CT: Yale University Press.

Kelly, G. A. (1955). *A psychology of personal constructs.* New York: Norton.

Klinger, E. (1977). *Meaning and void.* Minneapolis: University of Minnesota Press.

Lewin, K. (1951). *Field theory in social science.* New York: Harper.

MacLean, P. D. (1990). *The triune brain in evolution: Role in paleocerebral functions.* New York: Plenum Press.

Maddock, R. C., & Fulton, R. L. (1995). *The silent side of communication.* Des Moines, IA: American Media.

Maddock, R. C., & Fulton, R. L. (1996). *Marketing to the mind: Right brain strategies in advertising and marketing.* Westport, CT: Quorum Books.

Maslow, A. H. (1970). *Motivation and personality* (2nd ed.). New York: Harper & Row.

McClelland, D. C., Atkinson, J. W., Clark, R. A., & Lowell, E. L. (1953). *The achievement motive.* New York: Appleton.

Mischel, W. (1973). Toward a cognitive social learning reconceptualization of personality. *Psychological Review 80*, 252–283.

Morris, D. (1967). *The naked ape: A zoologist's study of the human animal.* New York: McGraw Hill.

Norem, J. K., & Cantor, N. (1986). Anticipatory and post-hoc cushioning strategies: Optimism and defensive pessimism in "risky" situations. *Cognitive Therapy and Research 10*, 347–362.

Olds, J., & Milner, P. (1954). Positive reinforcement produced by electrical stimulation of septal area and other regions of the rat bran. *Journal of Comparative Physiological Psychology 47*, 419–427.

Piaget, J. (1970). Piaget's theory. In P. H. Mussen (Ed.). *Carmichael's manual of child psychology* (3d ed., Vol. 1, pp. 703–732). New York: Wiley.

Rosenthal, R., & Jacobsen, L. (1968). *Pygmalion in the classroom: Teacher expectancies and pupil's intellectual development.* New York: Holt, Rinehart & Winston.

Rotter, J. B. (1954). *Social learning and clinical psychology.* Englewood Cliffs, NJ: Prentice-Hall.

Scheier, M. F., & Carver, C. S. (1992). Effects of optimism on psychological and physical well-being: Theoretical overview and empirical update. *Cognitive Therapy and Research 16*, 201–228.

Taylor, M. H. (1988). *The neuropsychiatric mental status examination.* New York: PMA Publishing.

Tolman, E. C. (1932). *Purposive behavior in animals and men.* New York: Appleton-Century-Crofts.

Vroom, V. H. (1964). *Work and motivation.* New York: Wiley.

Chapter 6

Neurological Substrates of Motivation

SENSORY AND EMPIRICAL SUBSTRATES OF MOTIVATION

In this chapter, we explore the neurological basis for the motivational approach outlined in this book. In chapter 5, we presented an empirical basis. This chapter offers substantial support for the localization of the motives that we have discussed within certain areas of the brain. In addition, the factor analysis has also given support to the ten elements that are an integral part of the Spiritual Survival Motive. In *Marketing to the Mind* (Maddock & Fulton, 1996), we showed that the motives themselves have substantial empirical support, particularly the two major motives that appear to account for the most variance, personal orientation and spiritual survival.

The problem with the whole topic of motivation as well as leadership is that they are *constructs*. A construct is an invented word used to describe basically what cannot be seen, measured or objectively defined. No two people would agree on a definition for the words leadership or motivation. Because psychologists and managers deal to a large extent with concepts that cannot be directly observed, they have to rely on the notion of constructs. Examples of constructs from psychiatry and psychology are intelligence, personality, ego and mental status. Examples of constructs from the field of management are leadership, motivation and training. All of these concepts are called constructs because it would be difficult to get two or three people who work together to agree on the definitions of these terms.

Critics, particularly behavior-oriented psychologists, will say that constructs are not verifiable and therefore have only limited use-fulness. However, in the absence of constructs we are left only with behavior, which in terms of an explanatory device leaves much to be desired. We have already seen in previous chapters that attempts to define leadership in terms of behavior alone would be simplistic, deficient and naive. There is much more to it than that. To make use of these motivational constructs that have been introduced—survival, orientation, leadership and so on—we must give some support to their actual existence so that they may be used in the design and perfection of motivation and leadership. In other words, we must show that they are real.

Constructs, such as the ones we are concerned with here, can never be proven. Scientists may verify hypotheses, but they never prove them. That the world is round, not flat, is a strongly verified hypothesis. So, too, is the evolution of species. There is little doubt about these phenomena. But the reason there is little doubt is because of the support that has been gathered over the years, not necessarily because of proof. The manifestation of evidence has been improved, but not proven.

Support for the motivational constructs introduced in chapter 3 is presented here, where we discuss sensory support; and in chapter 5, where we discuss substantive empirical support for the critical elements that operationally define spiritual survival. As previously mentioned, empirical support for the eleven motives uncovered in our research has been reported elsewhere (Maddock & Fulton, 1996). Sensory support arises from many experiments that have been conducted over the last 100 years on the brains of humans and animals. These experiments uncovered, either accidentally or purposely, the brain centers of emotion and motivation. Empirical support for these motives is derived from our own research in which respondents were asked to fill out lifestyle questionnaires, and then the motives were verified using the method of factor analysis. Further support is presented in subsequent chapters, which describe the results of our research with consumers and other groups who participated in our research.

THE NATURE/NURTURE CONTROVERSY

Psychologists, particularly behavior-oriented psychologists, have been strongly influenced by the philosophies of John Locke, who believed that the mind was a "blank slate" and that learning started at birth (or perhaps shortly before). For these psychologists, learning is the key to understanding the mind, as well as to understanding motivation and emotion. But the work of Piaget and others, which was described in chapter 3, as well as the current findings in the area of biogenetics, leads most people to question if not seriously doubt the blank slate approach to epistemology and knowledge. Although no proof has been offered, there certainly is a growing body of support for an "innate" factors theory. Nowhere is this difference seen more clearly than in the debates between Chomsky (1968) and Skinner (1987).

In U.S. psychology, behaviorism has controlled research and knowledge at least since Watson's campaign in 1912, when he said that "behaviorists have reached the conclusion that they will drop from their scientific vocabulary all subjective terms such as sensation, perception, image, desire, purpose and even thinking and emotion as they were subjectively defined." As a result of this crusade, nurture won out over nature and many of the vital "cognitive" components of behavior were ignored. Experimental psychologists, as well as other academics, performed experiments in recall and recognition because learning was believed to be the basis for all behavior. Particularly in the area of neuropsychology, almost all the research that was carried out was in the tradition of learning and learning theory. Investigators would create lesions in a section of the brain of a lab rat and then observe the results of those lesions on running a maze or engaging in a problem-solving task. The genetic or innate factors were virtually ignored. As a result, emotion and motivation, which we consider the most significant ingredients in their work, were overlooked almost entirely. This is unfortunate, for when emotion is left out of the picture we are left with no effective way to motivate people and leadership becomes just a constellation of traits and behaviors. Furthermore, people who rely on an understanding of motivation are also left without a road map. When they completed basic classes in psychology, it left them with a feeling of disappointment and a belief that they did not have the tools they needed for problem solving—certainly not the ones they were looking for when they signed up for the course.

SENSORY SUPPORT

One very comprehensive and exhaustive resource on the subjective (emotional/affective) origins of behavior is found in MacLean (1990). Hopefully this will be a harbinger. As he stated in the opening pages of his book, "no measurements obtained by the hardware of the exact sciences are available for comprehension without undergoing the subjective transformation by the 'software' of the brain" (p. 5).

MacLean presented a discussion of the brain that specifically deals with the subjective self and its relations to the outer, external environment. In doing so, he relied on extensive experimentation, his own and others,' that has been carried out with the brain and the nervous system. What makes his research and his interpretations of others' research so unique is that he focused on the origins of the subjective (emotions) rather than the objective (learning). As he noted, philosophers and psychologists have studied the problem of epistemology, but in doing so have virtually ignored the brain.

THE TRIUNE BRAIN

MacLean (1990) relied on explanations that depend heavily on the evolutionary development of the brain. In cross-section, he showed that it can clearly be seen that the human forebrain expands along the lines of three basic formations that anatomically and biochemically reflect an ancestral relationship, respectively, to reptiles, early mammals and late mammals. The three formations are labeled *Reptilian* (lower), *Paleomammalian* (limbic system) and *Neomammalian* (forebrain, cerebral cortex and cerebellum).

MacLean stated that these three divisions are responsible for three different mentalities and, as such, give rise to emotions and emotional behaviors that can be traced back in time to ancestral sources. MacLean warned that these are not autonomous brains, but instead used the term *Triune* from the Greek, which means operating independently but at the same time interlocked and functioning together.

Nonverbal behavior is an example of how one of the lower brains is involved in human behavior. Although animals cannot talk, no one would doubt that they communicate nonverbally. However, a very large part of human communication is also nonverbal, but because talking is so prominent in communication, the nonverbal part is often ignored. Usually the speaker supports his or her verbal message with nonverbal gestures and movements (Fulton & Maddock, 1995). This is an example of the Neomammalian (cortex) and Paleomammalian brains working in concert with one another. As Mac-Lean noted, the evolutionary study of neural architecture is a wholistic rather than a fragmented approach.

EMOTIONS AND THE BRAIN

In a study of human emotion, the forebrain dominates most of the discussion. LeDoux (1994) presented evidence showing that the limbic system of the midbrain, as well as the Reptilian or "R-complex" (lower) brain, are intimately involved in the expression of emotion. Recent experimentation and research with neurotransmitters and with the structures of the limbic system have had very positive results, especially in the chemical treatment of depression and other emotional disorders. Surely animals have emotions. But as LeDoux showed, although the limbic system, which consists of the amygdala, hippocampus and hypothalamus, is instrumental in the expression of emotion, much more is involved. MacLean (1990) stated that the limbic system has the function of "turning up and down the volume" or intensity of the emotions, whereas the forebrain handles the actual expression of emotion in the human animal and in many lower animals. As a result, this discussion as it relates to leadership focuses almost entirely on the role of the forebrain in mediating the emotions.

THE FRONTAL LOBOTOMY

Perhaps the most well-known fictionalized account of the frontal lobotomy was presented in the book *One Flew Over the Cuckoo's Nest* (Kesey, 1962). In the book and in the subsequent screenplay, a sociopath (played by Jack Nicholson in the movie) was accused of being a community nuisance and was taken to a state psychiatric hospital. Because of the charm that is usually associated with the sociopathic personality, he commanded the respect of all the patients. He organized them to go on field trips and boating expeditions, and, to the dismay of many of the staff, some of the patients began to show substantial improvement as a result of his leadership. However, because he was oppositional and virtually ignored all rules, he disturbed the routine of the hospital and eventually was given shock treatments. When those did not work, a prefrontal lobotomy was performed. As the writer and the screenplay tried to imply, this surgical procedure changed everything, and he became a "different person," quiet, retiring, dull, unmotivated, and fully compliant with hospital routine and regulations. More importantly, the patients who followed his lead went back to being "sick" and "helpless." He became one of them, and quietly settled into the routine of being "sick" with them and behaving the way hospitalized mental patients are supposed to behave, in accordance with the norms.

In an actual (not fictitious), well-known example, a prefrontal lobe injury incurred by a railroad worker named Phineas Gage was reported by Harlow in 1848. This twenty-five-year-old man was tamping with a tamping iron a charge of powder that suddenly exploded and drove the tamping iron upward through his left cheek and out the top of his skull. He was able to walk away from the accident and talk about what happened.

Recovery from the injury took about three months. After that time, he returned to work, but his co-workers noticed striking differences. Whereas Gage had once been a steady and reliable worker, he had become profane, undependable, fitful and impatient. He would not take advice. He was rude to other people. But most importantly, he also became a "drifter." Although steady and reliable prior to the accident, he now drifted aimlessly about, at one time going to South America and then back to California, where he died of seizures twelve years after the accident.

The importance of Gage's prefrontal lobotomy is obvious. But for purposes of the Silent Side of motivation, it is especially important because it speaks directly to the four Orientation Motives: Person, Place, Time, and, to a lesser extent, Circumstances. Gage's co-workers described him as a different person. Indeed, this is how patients who have undergone this surgical procedure are described afterward by their relatives and friends.

In terms of orientation to place and time, Gage had been a responsible worker and remained on his job, in one place, for several years. But after the accident, he drifted from place to place. Although most people who undergo this procedure are aware of the need to work, they do not express any urgency (time orientation) in finding employment. Most noticeable in Gage and others with prefrontal lobotomies, is a lack of commitment to planning and organizing, as they seem to have no goals or direction, instead wandering aimlessly about with little if any ambition or aspiration. This example suggests that the motives we have described as orientation are integral to functioning as we know it, and are destroyed, partially or wholly, when damage is sustained to the prefrontal lobes, particularly to the prefrontal granular cortex. When damage occurs for whatever reason, behavior changes very drastically. But the reason behavior changes is because there is a basic change in motivation.

Because we already compared the disorientation status in person, place, time and circumstances in patients with Alzheimer's disease, it is appropriate to look at other experiments that have been conducted. MacLean reviews the 1876 work of Ferrier, who decerebrated the frog. Following this procedure, he noted that the frog would simply sit and stare, motionless: "it remained fixed and immovable. It had no physical or psychic suffering, desire or interest. Surrounded by food, it will die of starvation, unless fed artificially"

(p. 22). Ferrier could well have been describing a patient with Alzheimer's in the final stages of the disease, where all phases of the Orientation Motives have been completely lost, including personal Orientation, which is always the last of the four Orientation Motives to be lost.

Procedures undertaken by Freeman and Watts in 1944 and described by MacLean (1990), involved incisions that were made on the prefrontal lobe. The patient appears quite unchanged following incisions on the first and second quadrants of the frontal lobe. However, after the third quadrant is sectioned, the patient's responses are diminished to one- and two-word replies, and after the fourth quadrant, the patient becomes basically unresponsive, except to urgent questions. Also, these patients are expressionless, monosyllabic and there is a *complete loss of orientation*, which is consistent with the symptoms of Alzheimer's disease.

THE EXPECTATION MOTIVE

There is considerable evidence that, as prefrontal damage is incurred by patients, the ability to deal with the future is also severely impaired. After all, the human animal is the only animal that has the capacity to chart and plan the future, or expectation. As MacLean stated:

> The *psychological explanation* in question is based on the inferred special capacity of the granular frontal cortex to anticipate the nature of future experience on the basis of past and ongoing experience. . . . Manifestations following frontal lobotomy indicate that the granular frontal cortex is implicated generally in functions related to an anticipation of, and preparation for, future experience in light of past and ongoing experience. (pp. 531–533)

It would follow that if the planning function was interrupted by prefrontal lesions, the Expectation Motive would be involved. According to MacLean, this motive involves "intuitive calculation" and has a close relationship to the Time Orientation Motive. He stated that these calculations involve both long- and short-term planning. An example of short-term planning would be that of an outfielder calculating the angle and distance of a fly ball and then making the catch. The example MacLean gave of long-term planning is a South Sea Islander who walks to the shore, raises a wet finger to the wind, and then navigates a boat to a pinpoint island 50 miles away.

THE ADAPTATION MOTIVE

We have not attempted to localize the Adaptation Motive, simply because it is already well documented. The Adaptation Motive is seen in diagnostic ultrasound during the third trimester when the infant moves his or her hands up to the face and continues to do so after birth for about six months. This is primarily a motor activity and, from what we can determine, functions to help the fetus adapt to the inuterine environment. After birth, adaptation is seen in ducks, which imprint on their mother immediately after hatching, or on the first moving object that they see if the mother is removed (Lorenz, 1935). Although imprinting does not occur in humans, neonates do establish a very strong bond or attachment on their mothers, or to whomever serves as the primary caregiver.

According to MacLean (1990), the function of maternal communication may be assigned to the Paleomammalian brain. With the evolution of the limbic system, three types of behavior occurred that were not common to reptiles: (a) nursing in conjunction with maternal care, (b) audio-vocal communication for maintaining mother-offspring contact, and (c) play. So it might be that what we are referring to as the all-encompassing Adaptation Motive resides in the limbic system because it is unique to mammals and is observed even before birth. But soon after birth, this motive converts to the innate tendency to "follow the leader" (imitation) and remains that way throughout the rest of our lives. This is an abrupt transition, and the two behaviors do not seem to be that closely connected. Bandura (1977), who wrote in the behaviorist tradition, would see this motive as a lifelong learning phenomenon and not an innate, emotional occurrence.

THE SURVIVAL MOTIVES: SPIRITUAL, PHYSICAL, TERRITORIAL AND SEXUAL

Because even the lowest of organisms are concerned with the day-to-day effort to survive, Survival Motives must be considered basic to all species and therefore originating in the Reptilian brain. These include the functions of physical, sexual and territorial survival, along with reproduction, mating rituals, and the continuing search for food, air and water. At the level of the human animal, this may include spiritual survival, which by definition cannot be assigned as a motive to animals.

But according to MacLean (1990), experiments since the 1940s suggest that these thymogenic functions also arise from the limbic system (Paleomammalian), which has three main divisions. The two older divisions are associated with the olfactory apparatus (much larger in animals than in man) and are closely associated with oral and genital functions having to do with procreation and self-preservation. MacLean (1990) noted:

> An analysis of the phenomenon of limbic epilepsy provides a basis for a classification of three categories of affects that is particularly relevant to epistemic questions pertaining to ontology, including a sense of time and space. It is of special epistemic significance that the limbic cortex has the capacity to generate free-floating, affective feelings conveying a sense of what is real, true and important. In regard to global functions, there is diverse evidence that the limbic system is essential for the interplay of interoceptive and exteroceptive systems required for a sense of personal identity and the memory of ongoing experiences. The phenomenology of psychomotor epilepsy indicates that the limbic system is implicated in dreaming and in certain psychotic manifestations. (p. 17)

Another indication that the limbic system may be involved with spiritual survival is in the transition to the three behaviors MacLean noted that were not common in reptiles. One of these behaviors involves parental responsibility to offspring, which is one of the crucial elements of spiritual survival and the one we labeled *family values*. MacLean also mentioned that psychomotor epilepsy provides evidence that the limbic system is involved in "feelings of self-realization, as evident by such experiences during the aura as feelings of an enhanced sense of reality, an increased awareness or self-duplication" (p. 578). Such feelings could come about in a drug-induced state, or could occur naturally with the excitement and revival that occur during the state of what Fleischman (1990) called "renewal and release."

In his conclusion, MacLean (1990) spoke directly to the phenomenon of spiritual survival in the "dichotomy that exists between the neocortical and limbic systems that may account for a dissociation in intellectual and emotional mentation":

> Moreover (and this cannot be overemphasized) the phenomenology of psychomotor epilepsy suggests that without a co-functioning limbic system, the neocortex lacks not only the requisite neural substrate for a sense of self, of reality, and the memory of ongoing experience [time orientation and expectation], but also a feeling of *conviction as to what is true or false*. (p. 578; italics added)

It appears in these references that MacLean was dealing with some of the most complex and abstract of thoughts, similar to what we called *spiritual survival* or what Maslow referred to as *self-actualization*. Yet, MacLean had an interesting conclusion:

> This presents a problem of crucial epistemological significance because there is no evidence that the limbic structures of the temporal lobe are capable of comprehending speech, nor is there any basis for inferring a capacity to communicate in verbal terms. Hence, it would appear that the manufacture of belief in reality, importance, truth or falsity of what is conceived depends on a mentality incapable of verbal comprehension and communication. To revert [to] a previous comment, it is one thing to have a primitive, illiterate mind for judging the authenticity of food or of a mate, but where do we stand if we must depend on that same mind for belief in our ideas, concepts and theories? (p. 579)

According to MacLean, there is a danger in overemphasizing the fact that emotion arises from the Reptilian and Neomammalian brains. This emotion, according to him, is known to be impulsive, vindictive, self-serving and protective; not altruistic, benevolent or generous. However in December, 1995—five years after the publication of MacLean's book, evidence was found for the first time of the probability of the nesting instinct in dinosaurs "and how they must have tenderly cared for their young." From *The* (Memphis) *Commercial Appeal*:

> The 80-million-year-old fossil is graphic testimony that the nesting behavior of birds today actually originated long before modern feathers and wings. . . . The sandstone fossil of the beaked Oviraptor, preserved with a nest and a brood of unhatched young, is the sole direct evidence of any dinosaur behavior, experts said. (p. 1)

According to this article, this fossil offers the first concrete proof that dinosaurs actively protected and cared for their young—"the strongest evidence of some kind of parental attention." Though nowhere close to the altruistic, patriotic, cooperative, loving and passionate motives that we understand today to make up the Spiritual Survival Motive, it does at the same time provide us with further evidence and confirmation of the strength and pervasiveness of what we are referring to as the Spiritual Survival Motive, even if in its most rudimentary form.

MacLean said that "believing such a motive could originate from the Reptilian brain [Spiritual Motivation] is therefore unrealistic." However unusual and valuable, this find might cause us to have to drastically revise some of our ideas about motivation, and particularly about the motive that we refer to directly as the Spiritual Survival Motive.

So, it is quite obvious that the Spiritual Motives that allow us to live together—love, concern, cooperation, patriotism and altruism—depend to a large extent on the neocortex. Without the neocortex, there would never have been a country as we know it, where law and order abide and justice is meted out fairly and evenly. And in cases involving disaster, like hurricanes or other natural calamities, people act impulsively, without forethought or anticipation, expecting no reward or recognition for their often heroic acts.

EMOTION AND INTELLECT

We often encounter individuals who are dumbstruck by the dichotomy that exists between rational and reasonable behavior typically associated with leadership and the emotional, irrational behavior that will occur within the same individual. How could a college president make obscene telephone calls to female students? How could an international figure in psychiatry have sex with certain of his female patients while they were under anesthesia? How could a respected and adulated spiritual leader spend his days off picking up prostitutes? How could a person who is well educated and from a respected family commit a heinous crime? The answer, according to MacLean, is that

> our intellectual functions are mediated in the newest and most highly developed part of the brain, while our affective behaviors continue to be dominated by a relatively crude and primitive system. This situation, I noted, provides a clue to understanding the difference between what we "feel" and what we "know." (p. 266)

REFERENCES

Bandura, A. (1977). *Social learning theory.* Englewood Cliffs, NJ: Prentice-Hall.

Chomsky, N. (1968). *Language and the mind.* New York: Harcourt-Brace.

The Commercial Appeal (1995, December 21). Nesting instinct find suggests dinosaurs tended eggs. pp. 1–3. Source: Hotz, R. L. *The Los Angeles Times.*

Fleischman, P. (1990). *The healing spirit.* New York: Paragon House.

Fulton, R., & Maddock, R. (1995). *The silent side of communication.* Des Moines, IA: American Media. (Book and video)

Kesey, K. (1962). *One flew over the cuckoo's nest.* New York: Viking Press.

LeDoux, J. E. (1994). Emotion, memory and the brain (Part 1). *Scientific American 270*(6).

Lorenz, K. (1935). Der Kumpen in der Umwelt des Vogels. *Journal of Ornithology 83*, 137–213, 289–413.

MacLean, P. D. (1990). *The triune brain in evolution: Role in paleocerebral functions.* New York: Plenum Press.

Maddock, R. C., & Fulton, R. L. (1996). *Marketing to the mind: Right brain strategies in advertising and marketing.* Westport, CT: Quorum Books.

Skinner, B. F. (1987). Whatever happened to psychology as the science of behavior? *American Psychologist 42*, 780–786.

Watson, J. B. (1924). *Behaviorism.* New York: The People's Institute.

Chapter 7

The Personal Orientation Motive in Leadership

BACKGROUND

Chapter 3 showed that there are two sets of motives in the non-conscious mind that account for a significant portion of human behavior: the Orientation Motives and the Survival Motives. In addition there were three other motives that we call *independent*: the Adaptation Motive, the Expectation Motive and the motive called Play.

People often ask which of all of these motives are the most important, the most "motiving" or the most powerful. But this is a difficult judgment to make. The answer to a question like this would be situationally dependent. In testing consumer products, we almost always find that very few products cater to all of these motives. Instead, there will be two dominant motives and perhaps two others that contribute to only a very small amount of the overall variance.

The Personal Orientation Motive is the one motive that appears to be the strongest in most of the consumer studies that we conduct. People want to know, when it comes to products, just how the product is going to benefit them, or, if it's a service, how the service can help them. They picture themselves wearing it, riding in it or living in it. This is the only way they can orient themselves to including this product in their lifestyle. They often close their eyes, turn on their "photographic" memory and *picture* themselves living in this house, wearing this suit or driving this car. When a consumer gets this far in a sale, it's very likely that he or she will purchase the product.

There are four Orientation Motives: Personal Orientation, Place Orientation, Time Orientation and Circumstances Orientation. When an individual gets up in the morning, the first thing he or she does before anything else, is orient him- or herself. Sometimes—particularly in the very early hours on very cold mornings—that is not an easy task. But once oriented, the individual pretty much stays that way, off and on, throughout the day. Usually it's more on than it is off, since that's the way it has to be. That special orienting device keeps us all on track; the same orienting device that keeps a bird flying north in the spring time and south in the winter time.

Just like we are not conscious of walking, we don't consciously tire because of having to remain oriented. But it can be tiring. And the whole rationale of vacation, weekends, escapes, and so on, is based on the need we all have to *disorient*. Hence the saying, "gimme a break!"

When we talk about the Orientation Motives, the actual motive is to disorient; to get away for awhile. This is because staying oriented and staying on task all the time, day in and day out, is—in and of itself—tiring and tedious. As we stated in chapter 3, even though when we see a disoriented patient with Alzheimer's disease we say, "Gee, I hope I never get that way," the fact is that all of us want to disorient or disconnect—temporarily—and then return to the real world.

The largest and most lucrative industries in our country provide entertainment, in all shapes and forms. Theme parks, the music business, sports, and television all provide disorientation experiences. Some provide these experiences through direct involvement and others by way of just watching.

The fastest growing industry in America is the gaming industry. In the extensive research that we conducted in casinos, we found that people frequent casinos because they think they are going to win big money. But interestingly, this is not the major reason why they visit. The first and most important reason for casino visitation is escape, disconnection and disorientation. Although this may seem hard to accept at first, it makes sense. Successful casinos have no windows. The lighting is very low. Mirrors on the walls and ceilings provide distortion. You will never see a clock in a casino—the only way to tell time is to wear a watch. When state law allows, drinks are on the house. The "music" is exciting, energizing and vitalizing. It has a beat (time orientation) but no discernible tune that would orient you to the music and away from the task of gaming! The temperature is cool to prevent gamblers from becoming overheated. Now what else do you need to disorient, or disconnect? Nature? Some casinos have that too—inside and outside!

Staying oriented all day is tiring and it takes effort—even though you are not consciously aware of it. So there is a robust motivation inside all of us persuading us to disconnect for awhile, even if it is expensive, and it usually is. Some more expensive than others. The whole recreation industry is built on this premise. The combination recreation–sports–entertainment industries are now the most profitable ones in America. The people who entertain are the highest paid in America. We spend more time being entertained than we spend working or sleeping. Disorientation and disconnection are big business in America and in most civilized nations today.

THE PERSONAL ORIENTATION MOTIVE AND SELF-CONTROL

There are many ways in which people can disorient or disconnect, and some of them were covered, very briefly, in chapter 3.

The Personal Orientation Motive is the one that accounted for the most variance in two of the initial exploratory factor analyses that were carried out on these ten motives. (The Play Motive was not included in the factor analysis.) Chapter 5 lists the factors, and the items that loaded on the factors. The Personal Orientation Motive accounted for 13 percent of the variation in factor analysis.

In chapter 3, we demonstrated that all of the motives have *elements*. Our preliminary findings on the Personal Orientation Motive are not only that it is the most robust of the Orientation Motives, but that it has the very important element or function, of *self-control*.

Shapiro, Schwartz and Astin (1996) reported an increasing agreement among clinicians, researchers and others that self-control is one of the most important and most critical variables involved in an individual's physical and mental health and well-being. They quoted Bandura (1977), Seligman (1991), Beck (1983) and others in saying that:

> Mental health well-being is associated with feeling in control of one's internal psychological environment (cognition, thought, and emotion) and its outward behavioral expression. Patients across diagnoses entering therapy make significantly more statements regarding "loss and lack of control" and "fear of losing control" than statements reflecting "having control" or the "belief that they can gain control." (p. 1214)

Although control is only one aspect of the Personal Orientation Motive, it is an important one. It is what keeps individuals on track, particularly when they are at work or functioning in an organization. As Shapiro et al. stated, it is an extremely important aspect of psychopathology and decompensation, but its presence or loss of presence is felt no less in individuals who are "normal," in the sense that they are not in treatment and do not have any physical or mental complaints.

Take, for example, a woman's declaration, "I have nothing to wear!" Very few men understand this, and when they hear it they respond in unison: "But you have a whole closet full of skirts, pants, dresses and shoes; what do you mean you have nothing to wear?" Very few, if any, men understand this statement, and the reason is possibly because when they ask their question, they usually do not get a response. What the woman really means is that on this particular occasion, she has nothing to wear that will allow her to present as the type of person she wants to present herself as at this specific function. In other words, a large part of the manner in which a woman maintains her self-control and thereby her personal orientation is in her wardrobe and how she appears outwardly to other people and not just to men. Although this is somewhat true for her male counterpart, it is not nearly as compelling. This is why department stores maintain two thirds of their dedicated square footage for women's clothing, and less than one third for men. A woman has many different ways in which or through which she can maintain self-control, in terms of the way she presents herself to others and also in terms of her personal individuality and uniqueness. All of this is part of the Personal Orientation Motive, which supports the fashion, cosmetic, hair styling, shoe, lingerie, haberdashery, skin care, hosiery and many other industries.

Cosmetics are another method of dealing with self-control that is incorporated under the Personal Orientation Motive. Adolescent girls first start experimenting with cosmetics when they are vulnerable to identity problems, primarily because of the biological and hormonal changes they are going through. Often they will use too much makeup, bringing down on top of them the disdain of their parents who will say "You look like a streetwalker. Get upstairs and take that stuff off of your face!" The child probably did not intend to look that way; she was just "experimenting." As she stands in front of the mirror she asks, "Is this me? Is this the kind of person I want to present myself as? Is this what I believe about myself? Is this consistent with how other people see me?"

When a woman wears a particular dress, suit or casual outfit, she actually feels differently about herself in accordance with what she is wearing. Similarly, the way she feels may dictate what she wears. Unpublished studies we have conducted in the past on women's footwear and hosiery products consistently yielded three types of women—dependent not on what they actually did for a living, but on their own personal orientation. First, there were women who were primarily oriented to being housewives and mothers. Second, there was a group of women who were primarily oriented toward sex and their own sexuality. Third, there was a group of women who were oriented toward management and business, and who were primarily interested in their careers. As you might expect, the shoes, hosiery and overall wardrobes of these women varied considerably between the three groups. Also, the type of personal orientation that a woman professed was not related to what she did during the day. A career woman's primary interest may be her family and children; a housewife's major interest may be sex and seductive activities. There was also very little crossover between each group.

OTHER METHODS OF SELF-CONTROL

There are many constructs that are related to the self-control issue. Bandura's (1977) concept of *self-efficacy* is related to the way individuals assess their own abilities to deal with forces outside of themselves; a sort of subjective assessment of competency. Seligman's (1991) concept of *learned helplessness* results from repeated exposure to elements over which individuals have no control. For some, religious beliefs provide a strong sense of control (Ellis, 1984). These are just a few of the many ways in which psychologists have looked at self-control, control of the external world and power as various facets of the control issue. But for our purposes in defining motivation, all these separate control issues are believed to be facets of the overall, all-inclusive self-control issue, which is part of the motive we call the Personal Orientation Motive. After all, the amount of control individuals have over their world will eventually be determined by the extent of their orientation to the world.

THE PERSONAL ORIENTATION MOTIVE IN MEN AND WOMEN

As Eric Fromm, a well-known psychoanalyst, observed, a man, unlike a woman, will usually define himself in terms of what he does for a living, his credentials or some other sign that basically conveys an economic value to the one who asked. A man might respond, "Well, I'm William and I'm a professional football player," or "I'm Richard, and I'm a dentist." For a man, basic personal orientation is summed up in what he does for a living. At parties, men often prefer to talk to other men. When they do, the primary subject of conversation is who they are and what they do—about their business, their profession or their livelihood, or about sports and play. Generally if you group all of these categories together, men are talking about *performance*.

If you listen, you will find that people—and particularly men—will talk in these terms. Sentences that begin with "I" are usually going to yield a cue about an individual's personal orientation to life. "I would never drive a foreign made car," or, "I work out twice a week" or "I have a six handicap."

A man's office will usually contain artifacts of objects that provide disorientation experiences for him: golf trophies, a mounted fish, vacation souvenirs, and so on. When a salesman or some other visitor comes in the office, these trinkets and other objects often serve as "icebreakers" by opening the conversation. Most salespeople feel that conversations like this (i.e., about personal orientation issues) are essential for establishing rapport and therefore making the sale. In some situations, however, the icebreaker can consume the entire visit, and when this occurs, it often kills a sale because the visit has no closure or "close."

The Personal Orientation Motive in women is similar to that in men, but not the same. We have already seen that women define themselves largely in terms of their clothing and what they wear. A glance at a woman's magazine confirms this. In no place is this more apparent than in a comparison to the advertising that takes place in men's and women's magazines. Research in this area has already been carried out by Farrell (1986) and is summarized here.

According to Farrell, a woman's primary fantasy is home and family. We are told that women have changed and that they now think in terms of management and career, but Farrell demonstrated that this is only on the surface. His "proof" that there has been no change under the surface is found in looking at the circulation figures of men's and women's magazines and the advertisements that fill them.

The largest selling women's magazines in 1984, when he conducted his research, were *Better Homes and Gardens* (1985: 8 million; 1995: 7.6 million) and *Family Circle* (1985: 7.1 million; 1995: 5 million). The largest selling men's magazines were *Playboy* (1985: 4.2 million; 1995: 3.2 million) and *Penthouse* (1985: 3.5 million; 1995: 1.1 million). Note that both of the largest selling women's magazines were in the area of spiritual survival, within the element we call family values. Conversely, most of the largest selling men's magazines were in the area of sexual survival, within the element we call impulse.

The largest selling magazines satisfying women's primary fantasy have changed slightly from 1986 to 1995. But only by adding magazines that are very similar in format and content to the list. For example, *Family Circle* has been replaced by *Good Housekeeping* and *Ladies' Home Journal.* However, the circulation figures for these three magazines differ so little that it would be more appropriate to say that all three magazines have tied for second place.

Farrell also said these magazines are designed to appeal to men's and women's *primary* fantasies. For women, the primary fantasy is home and family. For men, it is to have a beautiful woman.

For members of each gender, there has to be a way to obtain what they want, and there is, according to Farrell. Women get what they want (home and family) with glamour, beauty and attractiveness. Men get what they want by being the hero. Because of innate gender differences, neither men nor women can approach each other directly. A man cannot tell a woman he wants to have sex with her just because she is pretty or beautiful, and a woman does not get very far talking to a man for very long about how she gets turned on when she thinks about home and family. To a man, this conversation sounds like commitment, and that subject immediately sends up a red flag.

Magazines that appeal to this indirect or secondary need are, for women, magazines about beauty and attractiveness and for men, magazines about how to be a hero. In the women's category, at the time that Farrell did his research, the top-selling magazines were *Cosmopolitan* (3 million); *Glamour* (2.2 million); *Seventeen* (1.6 million) and *Teen* (1 million). Obviously, each of these women's magazines is about beauty.

For men, the top-selling magazines in 1986 were *American Legion* (2.5 million); *Sports Illustrated* (2.4 million); *Boy's Life* (1.4 million) and *Forbes* (.7 million). Farrell noted that each one of these men's magazines is concerned with being a hero: *American Legion* with being a war hero, *Sports Illustrated* with being a sports hero, *Boy's Life* with preparing to be a hero and *Forbes* with being a business hero.

Since 1985, all magazine sales are down, but the top-selling magazines for women's primary fantasy (home and family) changed only slightly when 1995 magazine sales were reviewed. However, in reviewing magazines that sell to men's primary fantasy, there were some changes. *Playboy* remains the top-selling men's magazine, but *Penthouse* sales decreased considerably. The reason for this decline may be the monumental increase in the availability of videotapes and other adult materials that satisfy men's primary fantasy more effectively and persuasively.

There have been some minor changes since 1996 in magazines that sell to women's and men's secondary fantasy, but again, they are only minor. For example, two of the top-selling magazines in 1995 for men were *Motortrend* (2.3 million) and *Field and Stream* (2 million). These appear to replace *Forbes* and *Boy's Life* on the list. However, the major point Farrell attempted to make—that the top-selling magazines appealing to men's secondary fantasy are related to performance—does not change with the addition or subtraction of these magazines. Indeed, the point he made is only strengthened (Famighetti, 1997).

Farrell made another point, and that is that all of the women's business magazines advertise the same products seen in the women's glamour magazines: cosmetics, perfume, clothing, and so on. Conversely, in the men's magazines, and particularly in the business magazines such as *Fortune* or *Forbes*, products for doing business are advertised, and clothing is secondary. This strongly suggests that the overwhelming motivational issue for women is the Personal Orientation Motive, whereas for men it is the Territorial Survival Motive.

Farrell believes in doing research on people where they spend their money, which is where we have done most of our research. Our findings are very similar. For Farrell, women define their personal orientation in terms of home and family and beauty. Men define their overall personal orientation in terms of performance, whether it is in business, sports, cars, toys or the like.

WHEN THINGS GO WRONG—AND HOW TO FIX THEM

The pyramid presented in chapter 3 defines human motivation. In factor analyses, these motives account for about 70 percent of the variance in human motivation. The way the motives appear in the pyramid is the ideal, but from time to time they are shifted. These "shifts" are related primarily to situations. For example, it would be generally inappropriate to proclaim your own virtues and attributes (personal orientation) during a church service where spirituality is supposedly of primary and immediate interest. Similarly, it would be wholly inappropriate to talk business (territorial survival) when visiting a person you worked with who is very sick and in the hospital (physical survival). This is just a simple matter of *ordering priorities*. So simple, in fact, that it goes without saying. However, these levels in the motivational pyramid can sometimes become very distorted and knocked out of place, and when they do everything seems to go wrong. A very simple example would be talking business (territorial survival) on the golf course (play). When motives get displaced in day-to-day experience and priorities need to be reordered in the pyramid, good, seasoned and experienced leadership comes into the picture. The leader is a motivator.

It's curious that it takes a grown man or woman to tell other grown men and women how to sell. They are called "sales managers." The job of the sales manager is to keep the salesmen oriented to the task (circumstances) of selling. Selling is a survival activity (territorial survival). The nature of most sales positions is that there are long periods of inactivity and boredom punctuated by short periods of closing, excitement and celebration. But it is difficult to stay oriented during these long periods of inactivity and inertia, particularly because the mind has a natural tendency to want to disorient. Therefore, it is necessary to hold meetings, have demonstrations, show videos and have visiting speakers to keep the salespeople on track and to minimize the possibility of disorientation. All of these activities are aimed at keeping these levels in the pyramid in proper order and perspective. This is because when they do get out of order and out of "sync," people lose their perspective and things go wrong. Here's what should be a well-known example.

JERRY MAGUIRE

The movie *Jerry Maguire* is about a sports agent, Jerry Maguire (played by Tom Cruise). Actually, this is a story about how the different motivational levels on the pyramid get out of place and cause major conflicts, until they are brought back into place again.

As a sports agent, Jerry Maguire worked for a very large agency that handled contractual relationships between professional athletes and the brands they endorsed. One day, in a dramatic plot point, Jerry Maguire is summarily fired by his manager during lunch. Following lunch, both Jerry and his manager dash back to the office and try to salvage as many of their clients as they can; the manager for the agency and Jerry Maguire for himself. It is a frenetic, passionate scene, in which Jerry manages to salvage one client, a football player for the Arizona Cardinals who promises to be loyal to him if he will "show me the money!" In addition, he recruits one clerical worker from the office, a woman who has been loyal to him in the past and who boldly announces that she will follow him, even though she realizes that he has little to offer in terms of financial security.

At this point, the levels in the pyramid shift. Previously, Jerry Maguire had his girlfriend (spiritual survival) and his work (territorial survival) separated. Now the two get mixed up because he has only one client on whom he depends for a living and that client is now moved up from the territorial level to the spiritual survival level. He literally worships him. His work becomes his religion, or his spiritual survival. And because his secretary was loyal to him, he dumps his girlfriend and takes up with her. However, this ambiguous sex–business–love–loyalty relationship becomes a hodgepodge of complications, mixed between sexual survival (impulse), territorial survival (business) and spiritual survival (love and marriage). Although they marry, she soon realizes that he doesn't love her; that their relationship was based on her loyalty and on timing (time orientation and territorial survival).

However, in another dramatic plot point, his only client (played by Cuba Gooding, Jr.) is injured in a game. For a few tense minutes it appears as if it is all over. All of the passion, commitment, concern and devotion that Jerry has committed to his client relationship and built his life around appears to be gone. And it is during this brief moment, as his life rolls out before his eyes, that he comes to the realization that the building blocks of the pyramid have been displaced or misplaced. They are out of order, and they need to be refurbished. And they are.

He goes back to his wife and reestablishes his marriage as a relationship involving spiritual survival and the crucial element of human love that is seen in Table 3.2. He then reestablishes his relationship with his client as one that is territorial in nature which, it always was to the client, who never lost sight of what it was supposed to be. Finally, at the very end of the story he reestablishes and redefines himself (personal orientation) as to who he is and his role as a sports agent. The building blocks of the structure of human motivation are once again put back into place. Jerry Maguire reestablishes his direction with clarity and purpose. He knows where he has been and where he is going.

A quick fix? Perhaps. In the movies the fix is always a quick one. But in life, this is the way that it really happens. The building blocks get out of order, and trouble ensues. Perspective has to be restored. The effective leader is the one who knows how to do this, and this is why we repeat our basic theme: The leader is a motivator. The leader is a person who knows motivation, and who knows that the only way to clean up a mess is to put the building blocks of the pyramid back in order again. Most of the trouble, conflict and turmoil that we experience in life comes from the arbitrary rearrangement of the motives.

Another example is when an executive falls in "love" with his secretary. Territorial survival, sexual survival and spiritual survival all become confused.

A career fireman sells Amway products in his off time. Then he begins to sell the products to other firemen on the job and to their families. Territorial survival and spiritual survival[1] are confused.

A salesman lands a giant account during a golf game, and closes it afterward at the clubhouse. He then gradually gets to the point where he attempts to play golf with all of his clients, on his time and on company time, justifying his activity as "work" (territorial) rather than as a game (play). Very quickly the golf game, and winning, becomes the end rather than the means. The motives get confused. It is difficult to close a sale on a golf course because golf is a game that involves total concentration and freedom from distraction and interruption.

And finally, there is sexual harassment; confusion between the Sexual Survival Motive (impulse) and the Territorial Survival Motive (career). These motives are so often confused and displaced that they have generated a whole new set of federal laws and guidelines, which are difficult to enforce because the evidence is so elusive. But here is another example of how the motives in the pyramid move toward displacement and disorientation and require repair and restoration. The sexual harassment debacle is an issue for leaders, not for lawyers. A business or an organization that has good leadership will never fall prey to sexual harassment charges because a good leader knows the levels in the pyramid of human motivation, and therefore knows how to keep the house in order. In other words, knowing what motivates people allows the leader to act and anticipate. To engage in *proactive* rather than *reactive* management.

LEADERSHIP AND PERSONAL ORIENTATION

As stated in chapter 3, leaders are people who are personally oriented. They know who they are, and what their mission and purpose is. They pursue it appropriately. What is important here is that once the Personal Orientation Motive is clearly defined, other motives often fall into line. The whole structure of human motivation begins to make sense—not only for the individual but for the entire organization.

For leaders, self-control is rarely, if ever, a problem because leaders have usually already defined their own personal orientation, which includes self-control. This is the reason why they are chosen as leaders, and could be considered one of the "traits" of leadership. Self-esteem is rarely a problem because this also has been clearly defined. Leadership is motivation. Living it and knowing it. The leader is a motivator.

As motivators, leaders also know how to repair situations that threaten to get out of control. Not only are leaders themselves personally oriented and in control, but they are capable of bringing others face to face with the reality of the nonconscious mind in terms of the structure of human motivation and emotion. Let's see how it's done.

Within each motivation level there are alternatives. Either a person is in control, or out of control, in terms of personal orientation. The same is true of, let's say, sexual survival. Either a person is in or out of control when it comes to the Sexual Survival Motive. Even within the Spiritual Survival Motive, a person can be either in or out of control. Each one of these levels defined as human motives can be either in or out of control. They can be either displaced or they can be in correct placement, in terms of the building blocks or levels of human motivation. When they get out of place or out of control, it is the leader who knows how to fix them. Simply because the leader knows human motivation.

COUNSELING

The word *counseling* has many different meanings. But in terms of leadership, the word or the process is very clear. The leader counsels with respect to the pyramid of human motivation, and the password is *perspective*. The leader's role is to help the individual bring the motives back into perspective again (assuming that they were once upon a time in perspective). Here are some examples.

One well-known example of spiritual survival out of control was John Salvi, who gunned down workers in two abortion clinics; one in Massachusetts and the other in Virginia (*New Yorker*, November 1997). Salvi's history showed a preoccupation with religion, but to a point that it went well beyond preoccupation. It became an obsession. His father said "If you are going to be fanatic, religion is not a bad thing to be fanatic about." But as it turned out, it was a very bad thing. In this case, religion (or religiosity) was out of control and spiritual survival was seen at its very worst. As it turned out, Salvi had a history of psychosis and schizophrenia on his mother's side of the family. It is interesting how often schizophrenia manifests itself in terms of good versus evil (control) and in terms of religiosity.

Alcoholism is a chronic problem within organizations. The purpose of alcoholism is disorientation, which we have discussed in detail. The alcoholic is not a sick person, as we have been led to believe; he or she is just a person who prefers to remain disoriented and disconnected from the real world of demands and pressures. But why should these people have that privilege? Wouldn't it be easier if we could all remain disconnected and disoriented, all the time, and not have to face the reality of the world?

In the past, many alcoholics have been given a choice between treatment or termination. But the effects of treatment have been marginal because those who treat alcoholics concentrate on the *disease* aspect of alcoholism. This approach only creates what Seligman (1991) called *learned helplessness*. If you are sick, you are helpless. So the recovery rate among alcoholics who are treated as sick or diseased is very low. We need to face the facts that alcoholics are people who do not like themselves and do not like their world, and so they stay disoriented and disconnected as long and as often as they can.

Facing the facts involves counseling with alcoholics about orientation and disorientation, not about sickness and wellness. Reality dictates that people stay oriented on the job. People who come to work with a hangover and make a lot of mistakes have an orientation problem and the solution is replacing the building blocks in the pyramid (i.e., it is a problem of perspective and orientation).

NOTE

1. Amway has products, but actually functions like a religion, as described in chapter 4. They have retreats, sing hymns, engage in "fellowship" and heavily rely on testimonials, in which people claim that the Amway distributorship has changed their whole life.

REFERENCES

Bandura, A. (1977). Self-efficacy: Toward a unifying theory of behavioral change. *Psychological Review 84*, 191–215.

Beck, R. (1983). *Motivation: Theories and principles* (2nd ed.). Englewood Cliffs, NJ: Prentice-Hall.

Ellis, A. (1984). The place of meditation in rational-emotive therapy and cognitive behavior therapy. In D. H. Shapiro & R. N Walsh (Eds.), *Meditation: Classic and contemporary perspectives* (pp. 671–673). New York: Aldine.

Famighetti, R. (Ed.). (1997). *The world almanac and book of facts*. Mahwah, NJ: World Almanac Books.

Farrell, W. (1986). *Why men are the way they are*. New York: McGraw-Hill.

Seligman, M. E. P. (1991). *Learned optimism*. New York: Alfred A. Knopf.

Shapiro, D. H., Schwartz, C. E., & Astin, J. (1996). Controlling ourselves, controlling our world: Psychology's role in understanding positive and negative consequences of seeking and gaining control. *American Psychologist 51*(12), 1213–1230.

Suiartz, M. (1997, November). *New Yorker*. pp. 90–107.

Chapter 8

Spiritual Survival, Leadership and Passion

BACKGROUND

Some examples of spiritual survival in leadership were presented in chapter 4. The purpose of this and the remaining chapters is to show how the various Survival, Adaptation, Expectation and Orientation Motives can move in and out of control at any time. When these factors are in control, an organization runs smoothly. When they are out of control, there is turbulence and disorder, and the emotions that people bring to work with them each day threaten to erupt and burn. As seen earlier in Ashworth's (1995) work, organizations cannot ignore the slumbering, evasive and elusive under-the-surface emotion that exists.

All of this presents an ongoing challenge to leadership. The function of leadership is to maintain and keep these motives under control. The challenge presented to the leader, as seen in chapter 4, is maintaining the perspective and the balance that is so critical to leadership, to organizational effectiveness and to the bottom line—whatever the bottom line may be.

WHY IS SPIRITUALITY IN THE SURVIVAL CATEGORY?

One often asked question is why the whole category of "spiritual" is placed in the survival category. In other words, is it really that important? Does it really belong there? If I didn't have a spiritual outlook or orientation, would that affect day-to-day survival? The response to these questions can be addressed in a number of ways.

First, the earliest discoveries and studies of man in history have always included references to spirituality, in terms of artwork on cave walls, icons on churches and cathedrals and holy wars that have been fought over the centuries. So despite the logical and scientific enlightenments of the 1990s, these wars are still being fought and it would be erroneous to try to cover the topic of leadership—or motivation—without including the topic of spirituality.

Second, we have already defined spirituality as being that about which people are passionate. Whatever impassions people is, in most cases, what they are willing to die for. This fact alone puts spirituality in the survival category. This is because people do die, every day, for what they are passionate about and what they believe in.

Third, our own factor analysis gave strong support to the notion that spirituality was a vibrant and robust motive in the structure of human motivation. It was found to be second only to the Personal Orientation Motive when measured in terms of the overall variance contributing to lifestyle.

Fourth, when we studied people in a clinical psychiatric setting, we confronted suicide and suicidal intent on a regular basis. As shown in chapter 2, Maslow's (1970) theory of motivation does not account for the phenomenon of suicide. For Maslow, physical survival was the bottom line. This means that spiritual survival is the most basic and the most controlling motivation.

Suicide is not a major killer of our population, but it did account for about 12 percent of the death rate in 1996 (*World Almanac*, 1997). In addition, there are many more people making suicide attempts. But these don't show up in the record books. So it is a factor that needs to be dealt with.

A little known fact that is now becoming more indisputable is that most suicide attempts that are made are by people who have been sexually molested at an early age. Often the abuse is "forgotten" consciously but "remembered" by the Silent Side. In our own clinical practice, 84 percent of the patients who attempted suicide had been sexually molested before the age of eight. This statement does not imply that it *stopped* after age eight, but that it started prior to that age, and usually continued. The suicide attempt generally occurs in adolescence, after puberty when sexual activity becomes a reality rather than just a possibility. In talking to these patients, who were often in compromising sexual positions at the time they came in for treatment, it became increasingly apparent in their minds that suicide was a trade-off between spiritual and physical survival. In their words, "I would rather lose my body than my soul."

The rationale for this can be found in the Piagetian (1971) approach to children's thinking. Drawing on Piaget's findings, particularly in his study of children's moral values, our own impressions and interpretations are that when children under the age of eight become involved in forced sexual activity with an adult, they will blame themselves rather than the adult, regardless of the circumstances. This sets the stage for guilt. In fact, this is where guilt comes from. Later on in their lifetimes, when they are confronted with the reality of sexual activity and performance, suicide appears to be the only way to ensure the survival of the spirit. This is not dogma, it is fact; and the fact is supported by national suicide statistics as well as the ones that we have collected in our own practice. Remember, animals do not attempt suicide; indeed, they do everything they can to avoid death. This is the point where animals and people differ, and the only way to rationally explain this difference would be in terms of spiritual survival.

SPIRITUAL SURVIVAL OUT OF CONTROL AND IN CONTROL

Is it possible that a person can be too spiritual, or overly spiritual? Is it possible that a person can have too much spirituality? It definitely is, in terms of the manner in which spiritual survival has been defined here.

Spiritual survival refers to whatever a person or group of people may be passionate about. When the word *passionate* is substituted for spiritual, one can become too passionate about a cause or a set of beliefs, and at times that passion can become completely uncontrolled. When passion becomes uncontrolled, the result is homicides, suicides and other crimes against people and property.

There are many examples of spiritual survival out of control. Some of these examples are post office shootings, Theodore "Unabomber" Kaczynski, drug addiction, alcohol addiction, church burnings, the "sexualization" of JonBenet Ramsey, various forms of terrorism, compulsive gambling, arson, serial killings, John Salvi and other anti-abortion fanatics and the Palestinian suicide attacks against Israel.

But spiritual survival is also seen in terms of passion, perfectionism and dedication in the opposite direction. Examples of this would be the discovery by Peter Doherty and Rolf Zinkernagel of how the immune system identifies cells infected with viruses, for which they won the Nobel Peace Prize in 1996. Other examples include heroic acts committed every day by people who often go unrecognized, but who risk their lives to save others from fires, floods, crimes and other natural and human-caused disasters. One need look no further than the local police department for this kind of data.

When spiritual survival is in a positive direction, as in the case when it leads to receiving a Nobel Peace Prize, it is well under control. When it is in a negative direction, as in the case of Kaczynski, it is out of control. Either way, spiritual survival—and indeed, all of the motives seen in the pyramid of human motivation—are ordered on a continuum from positive to negative or from good to bad. This is where values and motivation come together, and values are based on our capacity for making judgments.

At some point in almost everyone's life, there has been a judgment about what they are committed to, what they are passionate about and what they value above all else. Is it work? Family? Clubs and extracurricular activities? Sports? Some make this commitment early in life, and some much later. Some never do it, and waver and vacillate through life's journey never having made any kind of a commitment at all. These are the people who end up watching others as they receive the prizes for their dedication and zeal and the recognition and ovations for what they have done.

Spiritual survival is not a theoretical concept; it is real. According to the factor analysis we carried out, it is a viable and practical motive that explains a lot of behavior not previously explained. But it can work both ends of the continuum, and can rapidly get out of control. The effective leader understands spiritual survival both in and out of control, and that is what makes him or her effective. This type of leader understands motivation, and knows how to deal with loss of perspective in the overall structure of human motivation. This leader knows how to restructure that pyramid so that people and eventually a whole organization can run smoothly and efficiently without interruption.

PLOT POINTS

According to Field (1994), every screenplay must have a plot point. A plot point is a turning point in the drama in which there is a sudden and unexpected turn in the normal chain of events. Its purpose, according to Field, is to "move the drama forward, towards resolution" (p. 12). In a made-for-television drama, a plot point must occur during the first thirty minutes of the drama and again within the last sixty minutes. Otherwise, the plot will be very dull and viewers will lose interest and change to another channel.

Field said the plot point is part of the *paradigm*. The paradigm is the structure that gives direction to a plot or scheme. Field compared it to a road map. He stated that when one drives across the great reaches of some of America's western states all that can be seen is the road ahead. But the road map allows the driver to pinpoint exactly where he or she is. It also shows the driver the beginning and the end. Without a paradigm, we would all be lost. In this book, the *paradigm for leadership* is the motivational structure presented in chapter 3. A paradigm shows individuals where they came from, where they are and where they are supposed to end up. When you think about it, these are the only really important things in life.

People have plot points in their lives. There are financial, marital, business and all kinds of plot points. These plot points, such as the one's discussed as being related to sexual molestation, are unresolved and usually lie dormant in the nonconscious mind until a similar event comes along and triggers the trauma, emotion and passion involved in the first event. This will usually create a survival crisis, or what is often referred to as a "nervous breakdown." This explains why one woman can get a divorce and suffer only minor depression, whereas another requires hospitalization, medication and shock treatment, and still a third may commit suicide. This also explains why one man can lose his job and go out and find another, whereas a second man will lose his job and go on a shooting or killing spree. In both cases—divorce and job loss—a person who has an initial *sensitizing* trauma that is triggered by a second, similar emotional trauma may go berserk. In the case of the person who does not get out of control, the likelihood is that there was no initial trauma; therefore, there is no loss of control.

This discussion about plot points is included because it reveals a lot about the cause of loss of control and loss of jurisdiction over our own impulses and motives. In a way, it is like a double dosage. It is important to remember at this point that the nonconscious mind has unlimited recall through its photographic or "picture" memory, so that these very early incidents—even though they have been long forgotten by the conscious mind—will abruptly trigger and give rise to the emotions that were involved in this first traumatic event. This is how plot points work, not only in the drama that is seen in movies or on television, but in the drama experienced as life.

Another word about how plot points and the paradigm work together. Both occur in real life and in drama. In drama, people have direction and have charted a course in their lives, and then a plot point comes along and changes all of that. Another word for a plot point may be *surprise*. Very few would doubt that in real life there are too many surprises. However, if an individual has a solid paradigm that directs him or her toward resolution in life, then the surprises are not as damaging and devastating.

In this book, we outlined a paradigm for leadership. It is our contention that when an appointed leader has a paradigm or a framework within which to work, there will be fewer surprises and fewer plot points. When they do come (and they will), the leader is a skilled mechanic and knows how to fix them. We look forward to plot points in drama because they hold our interest. But in real life we dread "rainy days" and other occurrences, such as major illness, and yet we know they will come. The paradigm softens the blow—considerably.

SPIRITUAL SURVIVAL OUT OF CONTROL

Compulsive gambling is an example of spiritual survival gone wild. In our own studies of around one hundred compulsive gamblers, there could be no doubt that this was their passion in life. In fact, it was more than their passion—it was their whole life. Compulsive gamblers don't eat very much, rarely sleep and very few of them ever have sex. Because many of them count cards and involve themselves in other activities that the casino management considers "cheating," they are unwelcome in the casinos and are barred. However, some of them have gone so far as to undergo plastic surgery to change their appearance so that they can regain entry into the casinos from which they were barred.

Compulsive gambling is an example of spiritual survival out of control, and although it can be treated, a positive response is rare because it consists of a spiritual and passionate commitment. Even for those who do overcome the habit, most will eventually "fall off the wagon" so that recidivism is high, as it is among alcoholics and drug addicts.

Workaholics are examples of people whose lives are out of control because of their compulsive love of work. They usually have no interests or hobbies and dedicate themselves 200 percent to their work. They work nights and weekends. They spend little if any time with their family. They immerse themselves in their work. As a side effect to this kind of frenetic and frenzied activity, they begin to assume a sense of ownership and proprietary rights in the company, which often has serious implications for theft, misunderstandings, resentment and other problems if not brought under control.

Theft in the workplace is often caused by factors just discussed. In fact, workaholism is the most common cause because most theft is not driven by need or greed. People who steal in the workplace are generally individuals who do not need what they steal. Instead, they are people who feel a sense of entitlement; they have not been properly rewarded for the effort they have expended. They may even feel they have been taken advantage of by management or ownership. The following example may help to illustrate this.

A twenty-eight-year-old woman worked in a medical office that had twelve to fourteen physicians on any one day. It was a very busy office. In addition, this woman was married and had three children, was an active church member and was also involved as an officer and active member of an international business women's group. She belonged to the local chapter of this group.

Because she had a very outgoing and dynamic personality, she was moved into a position of leadership and influence by the physicians for whom she worked. It was a unanimous choice. Similarly, because of these same characteristics, she was catapulted into leadership in the women's organization, and very quickly, at the national level, recognized as "Executive of the Year." One criterion for this recognition was her strong, penetrating moral and character qualities, which she no doubt had.

Moving quickly into two strong and visible positions of leadership—nationally and also at work—she was rapidly catapulted into a world of *surrealism* (see chapter 4). The boundaries became fuzzy and began to fade. She felt an unnatural and unusual sense of power and achievement, which she had not felt as a housewife, an employee or a wife and mother. As a result, and because she had always been in charge of collecting and depositing large amounts of money, she began to help herself to small amounts of that money, amounts she felt would never be missed. As seen in most cases similar to this, the smaller amount becomes larger and eventually it is missed. In this case it was detected before reaching large amounts, so that even though termination was imminent, for her, visibility was held to a minimum. Her employer did not prosecute because of their long, positive relationship and also because the woman repaid the money. She also made an agreement to enter treatment. It was at that point that we found the reasons for her theft, which was an act that for her was entirely out of character. She understood and totally agreed with the surrealistic nature of her world at that time, which was based primarily on her achievements. Because of her understanding and acceptance of these facts, she was able to leave treatment with the understanding and reassurance that it would never occur again.

There were several factors in this case that need to be considered. First, as stated, she controlled large amounts of cash in a time when medical insurance was not as common as it is today. Furthermore, she collected enormous amounts of money that would have gone unpaid for her employer, and was told at one time that she was entitled to a percentage of what she collected. This arrangement paved the way for a *sense of entitlement*, in which she was able to rationalize to herself that she was entitled to more because she had been placed in a position of leadership and responsibility but had not received an immediate increase in compensation for this new position. She rationalized then, to herself, that because she had been placed in two very important and influential positions of leadership, she was entitled to have more money than she was receiving. She was probably correct, but instead of discussing this feeling with the proper person, she merely helped herself. The feeling of entitlement plus the ambiguous and confused boundaries worked together to create behavior that was totally uncharacteristic of her.

There is only one plot point here. The plot point was not the rapid elevation into a leadership position, although it was contributory. The major elements of the plot point were the shading and fading of the boundaries that usually occur with leadership, and the sense of entitlement that allowed her to rationalize doing something that was entirely out of character. This is what occurs with politicians, religious leaders, corporate executives and so many others who impress us with their qualities of leadership and expertise, and then surprise us with uncharacteristic behaviors. For most people who have never been in positions of leadership, this is very hard to fathom. It lies outside of their paradigm.

In order to understand the problems as well as the opportunities that are afforded by the Spiritual Survival Motive, we would do well to look at a few of Fleischman's (1990) elements. One of them, inner peace, accounts for a significant amount of variance within the Spiritual Survival Motive.

Everyone wants inner peace. But the way it is achieved will differ considerably from person to person. This is where individual differences enter the picture. In the movie *Jerry Maguire*, it became clear when Jerry Maguire had his motivational levels confused. This was because the only time he found inner peace was when he was with his client. He visited him regularly, to the extent that the client recognized that something was wrong and asked Jerry about it. Specifically, he asked Jerry why he didn't spend any time at home with his wife. He asked him if something was wrong, and then came right out and asked Jerry if he had problems with his marriage. Jerry Maguire denied it, but then later recognized, when he went to put the pieces back together again, that he did have a problem. Part of the problem was that he was looking for inner peace in all of the wrong places. He felt that the inner peace he achieved through his work could be replaced by his relationship with his only client.

As seen in the example of the lady embezzler, ambiguity is hard for leaders to handle, let alone the ordinary person who is not in a leadership position. This is where spiritual survival becomes a large and important aspect of organizational life and development, and of leadership. Lawful order is one of the elements defined by Fleischman and placed by us within the category of spiritual survival. Without it, there is little if any control, and leadership gives way to chaos.

Lawful order refers to the fact that the world is a lawful place to live, because it is governed by laws and principles that ensure there will be very few surprises. A person who has discovered that the world is a lawful and orderly place to live is not hard to handle. It is the person who is still looking for this orderly and systematic pattern who creates problems for leadership and management. Generally, this is the person who has not found or established a paradigm in his or her life.

Although it is not our purpose to review all of the elements of the Spiritual Survival Motive in this chapter, a few have been selected for review because of their importance to leadership.

SPIRITUAL SURVIVAL IN CONTROL

Fleischman (1990) discussed two very vital elements of spiritual survival—a need for membership and the sense of calling or of being called (vocationally). He said these two elements of spiritual survival are interlocked. Like all the elements he discussed, these are universal needs that exist in both men and women and are not restricted, limited or specific to any racial or demographic group. In his terms, "human life has always lived in the media of cultural structures, like marine life in the sea." Membership is what we are immersed in.

But these universal needs or drives that we call elements are not restricted to the religious life. As stated previously, what we define as *spiritual* is not restricted to religion, but is related to whatever people are passionate about. Nowhere is this better illustrated than in the "experiment" that took place at Eastman, which eventually led to Eastman becoming the only chemical company to receive the Malcolm Baldridge National Quality Award (Milliken, 1996). It is now referred to as the "Eastman Way."

Management and employees at Eastman jointly agreed they were going to become "the very best chemical producer and supplier"; not by cracking the whip and eliminating jobs but by motivating employees, who would in turn create the quality. By copying from the motivational hierarchy in chapter 3 (although they did it unintentionally), the Eastman Way was created. The whole paradigm was created by paying close attention to these universal employee needs: the need for membership, witness significance (involvement of management) and calling. In addition, they used some reinforcement methods out of traditional psychology, and added parties and celebrations to celebrate "a job well done."

By defining Eastman as "simply the best," employees jumped on board and enrolled for membership, because they wanted to be on a winning team. This is analogous to paying $50 or $60 for a ticket and sitting through freezing rain and fighting off pneumonia in order to watch your favorite team in the season playoffs. Everyone wants to be a *member* of, or at least feel they are a part of a winning team. That's membership.

By letting employees know they were a significant and critical part of the drive for superiority in the chemical industry, Eastman fed the motive that everyone is called to something bigger and greater than themselves. This is the element Fleischman referred to as *calling*. One Eastman publication said "Quality is very much a people issue. In a respect driven environment, all employees work together in a spirit of fairness, trust, respect and teamwork." In other words, they created a culture that, from our point of view, was founded on these critical motivational elements: membership, witness significance and calling.

What occurred at Eastman was a far cry from Frederick Taylor telling Henry Ford that any input by the worker would ruin the system, and that workers would not respond unless coercion and bribery were used (Taylor, 1985). And results? We've already seen how it led to the Malcolm Baldridge award for excellence. Very few companies ever climb this high. Because of their experiment with excellence, Eastman ended up being very close to the summit of U.S. corporations that breathe the thin air of success and achievement.

Wilsey (1995) provided another example of an unnamed company that followed a similar route. The company's founder died and the family successor showed little interest in the business, as is often the case.[1] As a result, morale declined, key people left, there was very little supervision and eventually a feeling of desperation permeated the entire atmosphere. A temporary consultant was called in and gave the remaining managers the first cardinal rule of membership: "Ask your people. Everyone wants to contribute and participate, but you have never given them a chance." He then gave them the second cardinal rule of membership: "People don't want to be managed—they want to be led." They then went about the business of constructing a transition team on these principles, and ended up with a profitable company and with increased sales.

Humanistic psychologists love to illustrate the application of their principles to organizations with the following statistic: More employees leave companies because of working conditions, breaches of psychological contract and other personal or environmental concerns than over money issues. But it is our contention that this fact or statistic has nothing to do with humanistic principles. Instead, it is related to motivation, and particularly to these two key elements of motivation: membership and calling.

When a business organization is sold and new management takes over, the first thing it does is identify and isolate the people who management would like to see leave. Because of isolation, which is recognized as a very powerful psychological method, more old employees will leave on their own rather than wait around to be terminated. This saves new management significant money that would have to be paid out in severance if these employees were involuntarily terminated. Being isolated from other employees with whom one has worked is psychologically very painful because of the basic need or drive called *membership*. In fact, isolation is just a simple antimembership or reverse membership methodology.

SUMMARY

In this chapter we reviewed, redefined and in some cases reconstructed one of the two most important motives in the field of leadership. It is a motive that—from what we can determine—has never been addressed directly but plays an important role in transformational leadership. In terms of redefining, we showed why spiritual survival is a survival issue and not an option or an alternative. It is not subjected to whether-or-not, or to choice. It is a *given*. We may choose to ignore it, just as we may choose to ignore exercise or diet as a way of prolonging and improving physical survival. But the facts are still there.

One of the ways in which we redefined spiritual survival is in terms of passion, or extreme emotion. It can also be seen in infatuation, commitment or even obsession. Although psychologists have studied these traits in the past, they have never studied them *emotionally*; only academically and intellectually. Our purpose is to remove them from the academic or cerebral area and put them where they belong: in the area of spiritual, passionate and ethereal commitment. When we did this with patients, they began to get well instead of just better. When we did it with advertising, marketing executives began to think in terms of *explanations* (of consumer behavior specifically and human behavior generally) rather than in terms of *descriptions*. And now, as it is applied to the whole field of leadership, our goal is that management will adopt this framework as a paradigm in understanding the whole concept of leadership. If these motives are understood and adopted, traits can be eliminated.

Table 8.1
Simple Structural Design of a Leadership Program Involving Motives, Elements and Goals

MOTIVES	ELEMENTS	GOALS OF LEADERSHIP PROGRAM
Physical Survival	Salary, bonus and incentives	Recognize outstanding performance with incentives and bonuses.
Spiritual Survival	Witness significance	(a) Management involved directly in program. (b) Schedule one-on-one meetings between management and hourly employees. (c) Direct recognition of achievement by management.
	Membership	(a) Become part of one of nation's leading companies. (b) Become outstanding by being a member of an outstanding team. (c) Become the very best you can possibly be.
	Calling	(a) Do what you were trained to do. (b) Make a difference! (c) Become an indispensable member of a winning team. (d) Personally achieve beyond your own expectations.
	Wholeness	(a) Find out how it feels to be a key player. (b) Be somebody! (c) Receive the admiration and accolades of all of your peers and from management.
Personal Orientation	Self-concept	(a) Make use of abilities you never knew you had. (b) Increase self-respect and pride. (c) Enhance dignity. (d) As you come to respect yourself more, see a corresponding increase in pride and self-respect.
	Self-control	(a) Enhance and optimize your known abilities. (b) Develop new skills and abilities. (c) Begin to experience power that you did not know that you had.
	Resolution	Resolve outstanding issues with management and other employees.

But more importantly, there will be a *framework* or a *paradigm* for proscriptive leadership. Going beyond Bass (1985), we now know that the basic principles of transformational leadership are *motivational principles*. These motivational principles are embodied within the eleven simple but straightforward motives we propose, and have been supported by our research. But more importantly, leadership is made operational by the elements that exist within each motive. Here's how it works:

Let's design, very briefly, a leadership program similar to the one at Eastman. We want to design this at the highest level of the motivational structure in chapter 3 because the higher level motives bring quicker, more longlasting results. Therefore, we incorporate three very important motives: personal orientation, spiritual survival and physical survival. Table 8.1 summarizes how the motives incorporate the elements and then the goals that are expected to accrue by incorporating these motives and elements. It is not intended to represent a complete and operational structure, but serves only as an example as to how the leadership can be fashioned and fabricated directly from motives. There is no guesswork. When you know the motivation, you can design each program accordingly, and if you emphasize the correct motives, the results will be the same or better each time.

The motives determine the effectiveness of the program! The blueprint is complete! The leader is a motivator, and leadership is motivation! Leaders are made, and not born!

NOTE

1. This may be recognized as another one of Fleischman's (1990) key elements, *witness significance*. If the person at the top cares about what happens and talks to employees in order to get their input, things go well. Conversely, when the person at the top doesn't care, things rapidly deteriorate.

REFERENCES

Ashworth, B. E. (1995). Emotion in the workplace: A reappraisal. *Human Relations 48*(2), 97.

Bass, B. M. (1985). *Leadership and performance beyond expectations.* New York: The Free Press.

Field, S. (1994). *Screenplay: The foundations of script writing* (3d ed.). New York: Dell Publishing Co.

Fleischman, P. (1990). *The healing spirit. Explorations in religion and psychotherapy.* New York: Paragon House.

Maslow, A. H. (1970). *Motivation and personality* (2nd ed.). New York: Harper & Row.

Milliken, W. F. (1996, October). The Eastman way. *Quality Progress*, 57–62.

Piaget, J. (1971). *Mental imagery in the child: A study of developmental representation.* New York: Basic Books.

Taylor, F. (1985). *The principles of scientific management* (reprint). Easton, PA: The Hive Press.

Wilsey, M. D. (1995, November). Leadership and human motivation in the workplace. *Quality Progress*, 85–88.

Chapter 9

The Physical Survival Motive and Its Role in Leadership

BACKGROUND

The Physical Survival Motive speaks for itself. It was prominent in Maslow's (1970) hierarchy, and also in learning theory or behaviorism because it is common to the entire animal world. Humanists or behaviorists are correct when they say physical survival is a motive. Without it, many people would not work. This was perceived as a serious problem by many in our welfare system, and has only been addressed in the last few years. If the government is willing to pay people not to work, why should they work? The results were as expected. When people were paid not to work, many of them did choose that path.

The problem is that physical survival is a low-level motivator. Our clinical work and other research has shown that when physical survival needs are fully satisfied—or even oversatisfied—people can still be unhappy or feel hopeless. The example given was that even someone who has much more than they need in life, and who seems to have not only extraordinary talent but money, friends and every conceivable comfort, will still seriously at times consider or even succeed in committing suicide. Despite everything they had, they were still unhappy. So although physical survival is essential, it is not the bottom line. Physical survival is a necessary motive, but not a sufficient one.

Throughout this discussion, we dealt with the major motives and the elements that define them. For example, the Sexual Survival Motive was defined and described in terms of three elements: sexual gender, sexual inhibition (impotence) and sexual impulse. Physical survival is likewise defined in terms of its elements: food, air and water. There is a possibility that shelter is also involved in a discussion of physical survival, but this is included in the discussion of the Territorial Survival Motive.

Elements are emphasized because in the discussion and consideration of a motive and how it impacts on performance, it is necessary to be specific and not general. For example, it is not sufficient to say that a person has a sexual problem, because that tells nothing. The issue is whether it is a gender, impulse or inhibition problem. Once identified, a solution can be found. Also, from the viewpoint of the Spiritual Survival Motive, we are working with eleven elements, all quite different in their function. When we work with the specific element, we can be specific in solving problems and getting results. Furthermore, these elements help define the motive. Conversely, when we work with the motive itself, we get confused because the motive suggests a very general and generic approach, whereas the element compels a more specific and targeted approach.

THE ELEMENTS OF PHYSICAL SURVIVAL: FOOD, AIR AND WATER

These elements do not need to be defined. We already know what they are. They are the basic necessities of life.

Behaviorists have been very specific in defining and working with the Physical Survival Motive. For example, they reward animals with food and water for desired behaviors, and punish or withhold reward for unwanted or undesired behaviors. But they go much further than this. They set up complicated and complex schedules of reward, called schedules of reinforcement, with which they make predictions about which schedule has the best or the most immediate results in "shaping" the behavior they wish to see. To a very limited extent, this also works with children. For example, in speech therapy children are often rewarded for pronunciation and articulation with M&Ms or Fruit Loops. Reward has been shown to be effective in improving children's speech and articulation problems. But other than this, behavioristic approaches toward motivation have very limited and diminished applications. For example, patients in nursing homes, children in schools or other populations cannot be deprived of food or water for the sake of motivation. In fact, federal laws even prohibit depriving patients in nursing homes of cigarettes, although they do allow them to be rationed at a frequency of about one every hour.

Attempts to use behavioristic principles with children in classroom settings have also met with considerable failure. One reason is that they are immensely impractical. Behaviorism requires a very complicated system of administering rewards and also of recording responses. Very few schools have the staff or the time to take with individual students in order to carry out this kind of routine. The alternative for many school children has been medication, typically psychostimulants such as pemoline (Cylert) or methylphenidate (Ritalin).

In summary, attempts to work with people—children or adults—by manipulating food, air and water supply will not work, except in very limited and constricted applications. This is why behavioristic methods can be applied in laboratories or in academic situations, but usually do not work in the real world of motivation. They are motivators, but their usefulness is limited.

COMPARING THE PHYSICAL SURVIVAL MOTIVE WITH OTHER MOTIVES IN THE PYRAMID OF HUMAN MOTIVATION

People do, however, work for food, air and water. They also work for shelter; that is, to keep a roof over their heads. And for many businesses and industries, reward is used effectively in the form of a paycheck, which is doled out on the basis of a *schedule* of rewards (e.g., every two weeks, every time a sale is made, etc.) exactly as behaviorism said it would be done. This tells us two things: First, people will "work for food," and second, food is not enough to sustain motivation in the short or long term. The first finding needs no elaboration; the second does.

When individuals go to work, they demand a lot more than a paycheck. They want, among other things, certain guarantees of equality, comfortable working conditions, security, status, time off, benefits and many other articles and elements that management must provide in order to be competitive. In fact, employees assume that most physical survival needs will be met. What they are really interested in is the other motivational categories that have been discussed, and how they will be met or satisfied.

For example, they expect and require a defined *territory* within the area where they work and often become quite protective of this territory. When their territory is invaded or disturbed, they become angry and upset. Often this will lead the employee to leave the job if he or she cannot be satisfied. This emotion is related to the Territorial Survival Motive.

Employees expect to get along with other people in the organization and not to be continually hassled, badgered and aggravated by those with whom they have to work. This need or emotion relates to the Adaptation Motive.

Employees expect to be able to maintain their individuality and the definition of themselves, who they are, what they are and how they present themselves, with some limitations. For the most part, they want to maintain their own self-image and self-respect. This is consistent with the Personal Orientation Motive.

Employees expect to have time off, and not to be on call twenty-four hours a day, seven days a week. They do not always want to work overtime. This is consistent with Time Orientation and Place Orientation Motives.

Finally, employees expect to be able to maintain their own personal belief system, whatever that may be. If that involves Kentucky basketball, Cowboys football or classical music, they do not want that disturbed. Frankl (1963), who was in a German concentration camp during World War II, said the one thing that prisoners were able to hold on to, even after they lost their self-respect and self-concept, was their own belief system. He said that, try as they may, their captors were not able to remove this from their lives. This is consistent with the Spiritual Survival Motive.

In no way do we intend to limit or restrict the importance of the Physical Survival Motive. But we do intend to put it in perspective. Motivation consists of much more than food, air or water. The experienced leader knows this. The effective leader acts on it by incorporating all of the motives in the pyramid and then making certain they are kept in order and in an appropriate structure and balance. Without that structure and balance, leadership collapses.

PHYSICAL SURVIVAL: SHORT TERM AND LONG TERM

One of the ways we test addiction is by withholding the substance to which the person is addicted. Alcoholics will typically claim they are not addicted to alcohol, and smokers that they are not addicted to cigarettes and that they could "quit any time." But when these substances are removed, the therapist may get an entirely different picture of whether the person is actually addicted.

As already discussed, we cannot remove the elements of physical survival. We know that physical survival is a motive; that goes without saying. But the manifestation and the strength of this motive vary from one person to another. This is what we refer to as *individual differences*.

In the 1970s and early '80s, physical survival was taken for granted and not often discussed. However, by the mid-1980s people in general began to become conscious of the air they breathed, the water around them and the environment in general. They began to think about what they ate—not only in terms of caloric and fat intake, but in terms of nutrition. And because of the meteoric increase in crime that took place during these years, they began to become very conscious of their own safety. Physical survival, in the last part of this century, has become more and more of an issue.

However, in some individuals the Physical Survival Motive is much more an issue than it is for others. The reason is that, at some point in the course of development, physical survival may have been disrupted. When this occurs, it often sets up a state of anxiety that is pervasive and persistent. Clinically, one of the ways that we were able to determine if the root cause of a patient's problem was at the physical survival level was whether we observed *anxiety*. If anxiety is the symptom, then an interruption or threat to physical survival is probably the cause of that symptom.

Conversely, if a patient presented with depression, the cause was usually in the area of spiritual survival because depression is caused by guilt. If a person is depressed, it can be assumed he or she is feeling guilty about something. It could be something that happened a long time ago, and usually is. Generally, the depressed person will make up things about which to feel guilty, but the root cause goes back to when the person's spiritual survival was interrupted, often by an unwanted and unsolicited as well as sordid childhood sexual incident for which the individual clearly and mistakingly blamed him- or herself.

Incidents that interrupt physical survival may include a near drowning, a near death experience, an illness or surgical procedure or a sickness that involves a very high fever.

Incidents that interrupt spiritual survival could be an unwanted sexual incident as explained earlier, or a death for which the person blames him- or herself ("I should have been there") or a major assault on the individual's belief system.

A person who is obsessed with physical survival issues may present as nervous, agitated, easily irritated, anxious and as needing a lot of reassurance about the future. The problem with this type of person, as most leaders and managers know, is that no reassurance is sufficient. This type of person is insecure, and needs ongoing and consistent reassurance. Because he or she requires continual reassurance, support and encouragement, he or she becomes very difficult to work with. However, the only effective way to work with these individuals is to assist them in putting the Physical Survival Motive back into place, or back where it belongs, in the pyramid of human motivation. This is actually the only way to work with anyone; that is, in assisting them with getting their priorities back in order again.

A thirty-six-year-old maintenance mechanic secured a position in an explosives plant. It soon became apparent that he was very uncomfortable working there and continually went to other employees for reassurance, asking about safety procedures. He avoided management because he did not want them to know of his concern. Some people in the plant were lax about following safety procedures, but never to the extent that the plant was decertified or lost its license to handle explosives. Nor was anyone ever considered to be in any danger. But although this employee started at the same time as other employees, eventually he did work his way up to management, almost insisting that the place was going to "blow up" if they didn't insist on enforcing some very restrictive safety regulations. Management complied with this, but that was not enough. He continued, which is often the case with a person whose physical survival has been interrupted along the way. Eventually, management had to talk with him about his own personal fears because they seemed to be so overwhelming.

What was found with this employee was that when he was about fourteen he had seen the movie *Jaws* and became extremely upset in the beginning of the movie when the woman who was swimming was pulled under the water by the shark, bobbed up to the surface about two or three times and then permanently disappeared under the surface. At that point, he began to have a breathing problem, claiming that he could not catch his air. He was treated for asthma, but the effects were minimal. He usually wore a surgical mask at work, which he said kept him from inhaling magnesium. He also had excessive absenteeism, which he said was related to his asthma. In discussing this whole situation with him, it was inadvertently found that when he was six he had a near drowning incident that required emergency room treatment and a short stay in the hospital. This is the event that interrupted his physical survival and also caused him to be so hypervigilant regarding the safety conditions in the plant. This is also why he could not be satisfied with the changes that were made to accommodate him. The problem was within the structure of motives and not in the plant itself. Management talked with him about this event, and for the most part gave him reassurance and redirection, assuring him that although the drowning was a close-to-death experience he did live through it and he was a survivor. Dealing straight on with the event that interrupted his physical survival and helping him see that he did survive was tremendously helpful to this employee, and allowed him to go

back to work with a significant decrease in complaints and absenteeism.

This brief illustration shows that physical survival problems are
often long term, not short term. They are *backdated*. That is, they
relate to a crisis that occurred a long time ago in a person's life, but
was never resolved. In chapter 7, we referred to these incidents as
plot points, comparing them with the plot points that occur in people's lives. The problem is that, unlike the plot points seen in television, book and movie dramas, these particular plot points never
get resolved. And so it is like an open wound that continues to swell
and exhibit inflammation. But because it is in the nonconscious
mind it is unrecognized and unremembered, thus a person who has
this problem will tend to blame his or her uncomfortable state on
things that are around him or her that can be seen and touched,
and that are tangible. In this case, it was the laxity of plant management and the failure to take proper safety precautions.

PHYSICAL SURVIVAL AND THE TRANSACTIONAL LEADERSHIP PARADIGM

Bass (1997), using the MLQ, defined not only transformational
leadership but also transactional leadership. He showed that transformational leadership is universal in the sense that it is consistent
with the ideals and prototypes that people have about leadership in
numerous studies that have been done around the world, on all
continents except Antarctica. But transactional leadership is also a
factor, because it is the style of leadership most common in many
situations. Transactional leadership is characterized by Bass as a
"carrot on a stick" approach, and consists of three components that
he viewed as instrumental: contingent reward, active management
by exception and passive management by exception. He also stated
that "people jockey for positions in transactional leadership,
whereas in transformational leadership they share common goals.
Rules and regulations dominate the transactional organization;
adaptability is a characteristic of the transformational organization"
(p. 131).

The first component speaks for itself: Rewards follow expected
performance. Based on this ingredient of transactional leadership,
it is quickly seen as a performance-reward system, which was discussed in chapter 2. As discussed previously, there are a number
of studies, particularly those by Kohn (1993a, 1993b), supporting
the findings that rewards don't work. It is relevant that many of
these studies have been done in elementary and secondary educational settings, where the children involved do not see physical sur-

vival as a motive. Conversely, in the workplace, physical survival is a motive that is always in the background, but nevertheless omnipresent.

Therefore, transactional leadership is a good example of the direct application of the Physical Survival Motive to a leadership paradigm: "If you work you eat." The second two components of transactional leadership are also consistent with this: active management by exception, where leaders enforce rules only when mistakes are being made, and passive management by exception, where leaders wait until mistakes are brought to their attention and then intervene in the leadership-management process. In many organizations, where fighting fires is the order of the day, transactional leadership is the management style of choice, simply because management cannot take enough time away from fighting fires to design any other kind of program.

Transactional leadership, then, is a kind of lower level management style that permeates most businesses and organizations, simply because it is a more "commonsense" style of leadership and therefore more easily applied. Like Maslow's (1970) hierarchy, it is simple, straightforward and easily remembered (Watson, 1996).

SUMMARY

The observation offered by Krugman (1994) in chapter 4 is worth paraphrasing here for the reader. According to Krugman, U.S. psychology has spent a lot of time looking at very basic and simplistic responses of animals and people, and have overlooked the big picture. We believe that, with reference to leadership, Bass said the same thing. But to put it into our paradigm, there is more to motivation than physical survival. And because leadership is motivation, there is more to leadership than the carrot on the end of the stick. Transactional leadership works, because physical survival is a motive, and all motives will work when it comes to goal achievement. But we have found in our research that the more motives that are working together, the more quickly the goal is attained, up to a point. After a certain juncture, however, there is a point of diminishing returns. The work that Bass and his associates have done in leadership certainly points to a similar conclusion. The more higher level motives included in leadership, the faster the goals are achieved.

REFERENCES

Bass, B. M. (1997). Does the transactional–transformational leadership paradigm transcend organizational and national boundaries? *American Psychologist 52*(2), 130–139.

Frankl, V. (1963). *Man's search for meaning.* New York: Washington Square Press.

Kohn, A. (1993a). *Punished by rewards.* Boston: Houghton Mifflin.

Kohn, A. (1993b, September–October). Why incentive plans cannot work. *Harvard Business Review 71,* 54–63.

Krugman, H. E. (1994). Pavlov's dog and the future of consumer psychology. *Journal of Advertising Research 34*(6), 67–71.

Maslow, A. H. (1970). *Motivation and personality* (2nd ed.). New York: Harper and Row.

Watson, T. J. (1996). Motivation: That's Maslow, isn't it? *Management Learning 27*(4), 447.

Chapter 10

Leadership and the Territorial Survival Motive

PROTECTING WHAT RIGHTFULLY BELONGS TO YOU

The appearance of Desmond Morris' bestseller *The Naked Ape* (1967) provided an amusing, persuasive argument that the territorial drives in animal species extend to organized human society. Our own diagnostics confirm that conclusion. In fact, territorial survival is one of the most powerful motives of the human nonconscious. As stated previously, most everyone has had the experience of having a neighbor who was an all-around good guy with a sweet personality who turns into the town crank whenever someone traipses across his lawn. The same reactions can be seen on a figurative basis in the business world. A corporate executive whose domain is challenged by company restructuring may react quite irrationally, possibly even deviously, to thwart the perceived invasion. Under these conditions, powerful emotions are experienced in the business world, even though most people agree that emotion does not belong in business. Territoriality is a major factor in office politics.

Territoriality is a universal, Silent Side motivation, but its exact nature is still clouded by cultural bias and sexism. Until lately, many believed that territorial survival was peculiar to men, not women. That mistaken conclusion was based on the aggressive behavior of males who dominated competitive occupations. Now that occupational barriers to women have lessened, it appears that females with professional careers exhibit the same Territorial Survival Motives as their male counterparts, almost. There are still some distinguishable differences, as seen in the differences in magazine circulation reviewed in chapter 7.

If magazine circulation is any indication of where our territorial preferences are, and it seems to be a legitimate way to define people's primary interests,[1] then the major *primary* territorial interests of men are still scoping out the territory and finding a beautiful woman, and for women the major *primary* territorial interests are in home and family. As Farrell (1986) stated, the way that women get what they want is by looking beautiful and for men it is being a hero. This leads to men and women's *secondary* territorial interests, and the magazine subscription statistics that Farrell found in 1986 and that we updated in 1995 also support these observations. For example, in 1986 the top-selling magazines appealing to women's secondary territorial interest were *Cosmopolitan, Glamour* and *Seventeen* (in that order) and for men they were *Sports Illustrated, Motortrend* and *Field and Stream*. The actual figures are reported in chapter 7. The findings are repeated here because they illustrate a principle that is very important when it comes to understanding and interpreting the Territorial Survival Motive. But they also illustrate another important point, and that is that although times change and things are different, there are still some major differences at the nonconscious level between the sexes. For example, our own factor analysis of the major motives involved on the Silent Side that was reported in chapter 5 showed that the Territorial Survival Motive broke out in two parts, one for males and one for females. This was expected.

YOU ARE WHAT YOU READ

There is an old saying that is definitely out of vogue and politically incorrect, and that is that "a woman's place is in the home." But the fact that *Good Housekeeping* and *Family Circle* are still the best-selling women's magazines tells us that there is at least a duality or a paradox in the territorial motivation when it comes to women. Fifty percent of women are involved in careers outside of the home. But even though more women are now in middle and upper management positions, there is a problem. We can assume a strong Territorial Survival Motive exists in women and their relationship with their career and particularly in dealing with the territorial elements of achievement, power and status. But women do remain motivated by other territorial obligations that men do not have. However, there is growing evidence that men also are beginning to experience this conflict as it pertains to territorial motivation. The conflict is expressed in both sexes as "Where do I really belong?"

TERRITORIAL SURVIVAL IS REGULARLY CHALLENGED

Territorial survival is more conspicuous than most Silent Side motives because it is regularly challenged by outside forces. When an individual's space is threatened, he or she usually reacts vigorously, displaying fear, anxiety or agitation. Then the resources at hand are mobilized to stop the incursion and, often, reverse the process. In business that is called the *competitive spirit*. Some have even observed that the defensive tactics used in competition are the same as those used in war (Bryan, 1985).

Because there is obviously a relation between territoriality and competition, further exploration of the Territorial Survival Motive may enhance understanding of competitiveness as a social phenomenon. Is there perhaps a parallel between childhood training and adult territorial competitiveness? The appeal of organized sports revolves around the Territorial Survival Motive. From early childhood, we all learn the importance of protecting a piece of turf with teamwork. That's not all there is to organized sports, of course. Fans know how the ballyhoo, ritual and general hysteria surrounding championship teams transcends territoriality and enters the realm of the spiritual. Ever experienced depression the day after your team lost a game? If so, you're spiritually hooked.

The Olympics is a sporting event that invariably shifts motives from the Territorial Survival Motive to the Spiritual Survival Motive by interjecting elements of patriotism and nationalism. An extreme case was the 1994 Winter Olympics in Norway, during which untold millions watched the figure skating showdown between Nancy Kerrigan and Tonya Harding, both Americans. The Territorial Survival Motive was altogether forgotten. Top-level, good-versus-bad, the Spiritual Survival Motive had totally taken over.

In the late 1990s, there is much public debate about media violence and its effect on children. It is too early to make a definitive statement on this point, but it might be that much of the aggression displayed by today's media-saturated kids is rooted in territorial emotions. So much of children's television programming and electronic games is structured around aggressive competition: violent struggles of opposing forces, bash-and-crash attack and defense, threats to security that are dealt with by super heroes, super bunnies, super robots, or whatever. Do such motifs twiddle children's inherent territorial emotions? Is there a long-term effect in kids? Someday we may know the answers.

Territorial differences between men and women are important and must be discussed and considered in any comprehensive discussion of leadership. Much of this is covered in chapter 11, where the Sexual Survival Motive is discussed in detail. Gender is one of the four elements of sexual survival, and in chapter 11 we consider the issue of gender differences in leadership.

CORPORATESPEAK: ACHIEVEMENT AND STATUS TRANSMITTED IN A WORD

The Territorial Survival Motive may be seen and understood in organizations by what is called *corporatespeak*. Certain words or phrases, or combinations of word–phrases, are capable of transmitting more meaning than they are meant to, and certainly more than the one-dimensional dictionary definition of the word otherwise would indicate. This indiscernible corporatespeak improves the growth of a company, or so it would seem.

A large, publicly held corporation had gross receipts of $3 billion by 1997. In the early '90s this was a $500 million manufacturing firm, which although outwardly successful, was barely managing its cash flow. In the early '90s, this privately held company saw its fourth CEO in five years. But this one made a difference! In a five-year span, he remedied the cash flow management problems and the business grew. He was able to borrow money, first from lenders and then from the stockholders as the company had a successful IPO. The money went from $500 million in revenue to $3 billion. Fifteen acquisitions and ten thousand additional employees later, a certain corporatespeak began to take hold.

Senior management began to speak in terms of *skill-set, conversion*, and *top-side*. The word *team* was bantered about with different modifiers: *team effort* and *team skills*.

For example, *conversion* started its life in the organization as a simple, one-word description of the percentage of revenue left from earnings by a profit center or total. As the company grew and the revenues (and challenges) grew, this word also grew and took on new meanings. It became a designator of who did and did not understand the intricacies of the balance sheet. Those not understanding the complexity of the balance sheet could never become members of the senior management "club." In all quarterly and semi-annual meetings, those who used this word correctly and those who used it incorrectly were observed by senior management. "Our conversion of revenue to earnings for the month was 12 percent." As this word began to filter down to the operating managers, they started to use it in code speech for good performance only. In other words, of the fifty operating managers who met quarterly in New York, only those who had operated better than plan would use the word *conversion* to describe their location's total performance.

The distinction became so obvious that it was used in polite conversation at cocktail parties to describe who would make their numbers each year and who would not.

The word *skill-set* also became very popular among senior management. Rather than talk in terms of one's capabilities, they would talk about a person's *skill-set*. "We are recruiting for a new position, and need an individual with the appropriate skill-set." The details of skill-set were never defined. By code, it meant that certain people in the room knew what was required, whereas the others did not know.

Top-side became a coded way of communicating the message "We're not going into detail here." In meetings with senior managers, *top-side* could be used to refer to a financial statement review of an operation as opposed to a detailed line-item review. It could also mean a review of a certain individual's qualities or attributes (skill-set). Only the most capable or strongest manager could use the phrase. Those who were not capable of using the phrase and who dared use it, soon found their way out of the organization.

The CEO of this corporation was fond of moving management from one assignment to another, and also changing the individual to whom they reported from time to time. None of the fifty to seventy-five senior staff remained in one position for very long. Hence, the word *team*. It had the connotation of a sports team, in which players were used in different positions. When the CEO used the word *team* it meant essentially a "change in position." Members of the senior management staff could predict from the CEO's use of this word who would soon be leaving, for their name was never mentioned in connection with the *team*.

It is inevitable that a unique language will develop in every organization, regardless of its purpose or structure. Members of the clergy will ask, upon greeting or seeing an acquaintance in a restaurant or public place, "Is he a church man?" Street gangs have their own language. Every profession has its own corporatespeak in addition to its technical and professional terminology that is part of the lexicon of the profession. This is especially apparent as one reviews hospital and clinic records in these times of managed care. There are certain categories of illness and certain kinds of treatment that are not allowed under payment restrictions. Therefore, these diagnoses and procedures are "coded" informally on the chart, so they meet the criteria of the managed care organization for payment, but to the professional who writes the diagnoses they have an entirely different meaning.

Corporatespeak and other idiosyncrasies in vocabulary and lexicon are essential in defining territorial differences.

TO WHICH TEAM DO YOU BELONG?

A three-hundred-employee manufacturing organization was in the midst of a wrenching turnaround. As part of this turnaround, a massive overhaul of machinery was undertaken, as well as an effort toward sales and marketing that totally saturated the potential customer base. There were also layoffs of salaried and hourly production personnel, as there usually are when a new owner takes over. Many volunteered to be laid off. Of those that were left, regular meetings on a twice-weekly or more frequent basis were held, explaining to them what was happening as progress was made. They understood what was happening and indicated that they were in agreement with the changes.

The turnaround was so successful, that six months after the sale the plant boasted better earnings than it had experienced in three years. Although a shut-down was considered by senior management at one point, the idea was soon discarded. Instead, management recruited new customers for the product, and brought in new equipment and technology and installed them at the location.

As the turnaround was in progress, the busy season for the plant came around. With almost half of the old workforce gone and one shift knocked out, the workload tripled. With that, employee morale sank to an all-time low, and this was inevitably followed by a push to unionize the plant. Although the plant's manager was a good technician, he was highly ineffective at articulating and executing change with people, and he was a noncharismatic leader. Management sent in the plant manager's supervisor to conduct twenty-four, thirty-minute union information meetings that would reach all three hundred employees. The well-prepared and delivered speech, by an individual who knew about and understood the motivational structure of the Silent Side, had almost instant acclaim. Most of the meetings ended with anti-union sentiment running at an emotional pitch. In fact, 15 percent of the workforce requested permission on the spot to be allowed to post anti-union posters and to circulate a "get out of town" petition to the union organizers. Following are some excerpts from this highly effective appeal to keep the union out of the plant:

> As I consider this union thing, I get upset. But upset for reasons that may not be apparent to you. One year ago I came in as we bought this company and made sweeping changes. As you recall, and as we told you in detail in meetings, we were heading downhill at that time. At the time of the sale we had lost $1.5 million. I also told you, and remind you today, that was not your fault. You didn't lose the money. The

problem was that prior management didn't manage. I am the one who told you this, and I am the one who laid off eighty-five people and changed the benefit package. But I also reminded you that hard work and dedication would keep this plant open, turn it around and make it grow. I also told you it would be difficult, but when we did it, you as much as anyone would be responsible. You would help us to manage it back to a healthy status.

It's now the busiest season. We've been at this turnaround for twelve months. We're profitable, more so than in prior years, but we're not quite to business plan yet. But we're heading there. We're on the threshold of landing a new account, a very big one. If we get it, it could mean new equipment, new jobs and most important, continued survival.

Where were these outsiders twelve months ago? Where were these professional union organizers then, who are paid to act as full-time salespeople and promise happiness? Did they come twelve months ago with customers to prevent the layoff? Did they go to prior management and offer help? If you were unhappy twelve months ago, did they approach you as they are now, offering to help in exchange for your dues? No, they didn't. You and I were doing the tough stuff. Making hard decisions. Laying off fellow employees because we lacked the work to keep them here. The professional outsiders are here now, because you are tired, since we are in the middle of our busy season. You and I have helped this plant to make money again. They're here to offer you promises. But they're here to prey on your fatigue also. I resent that. How dare they think that you are that shallow, and that you can't see through their selfish motives. Who are these strangers? Who are these professional salespeople?

This talk stirred emotions in every meeting, and there were several employees who shed tears because this manager had evoked emotion; emotion in the form of the Territorial Survival Motive. He spoke directly about career, income and competition. He talked about territory—yours and mine! He talked about every aspect of the Territorial Survival Motive because that is what work is all about. He talked about power, achievement, status and control.

This speech is included because it is an excellent example not only of territorial survival, which was the end result, but also of the positive use of emotions and motivation in business. Who said that emotion has no place in the business world (Ashworth, 1995; Cooper, 1997)?

NOTE

1. Magazines are vertical, in that they focus in depth on the primary interests of their readers. The old magazines that took a horizontal approach

to journalism (i.e., "something for everyone") have considerably less market share than they had in the past as their readers have moved toward specialty magazines.

REFERENCES

Ashworth, B. E. (1995). Emotion in the workplace: A reappraisal. *Human Relations 48*(2), 97–126.

Bryan, W. J. (1985). *The Chosen Ones. The art of jury selection* (special ed.). Glendale, CA: Westwood Publishing Co.

Cooper, R. K. (1997). Applying emotional intelligence in the workplace. *Training and Development 51*(12), 31–38.

Farrell, W. (1986). *Why men are the way they are.* New York: McGraw-Hill.

Morris, D. (1967). *The naked ape: A zoologist's study of the human animal.* New York: McGraw-Hill.

Chapter 11

Leadership and the Role of Sexual Survival

SEX AND EMOTION IN THE WORKPLACE

Ashworth (1995) revealed that emotion in the workplace has traditionally been limited to some very stable affective states. Such mild emotional events include whether people are satisfied or unhappy with their jobs, and the role of emotion in discrete critical events such as termination, reorganization and new management.

However, the 1980s forced organizations to take a more realistic and practical look at the role of emotion at work. In California, organizations began to experience a deluge of worker's compensation claims that asserted stress as a major cause of their work-related "injuries." Many of these claims came from workers in organizations where they would be the least expected: motels, bars and restaurants and the state itself. It did not take long for the epidemic of stress claims that invaded California to spread to other states, where a number of people saw an excellent opportunity to cash in on a compensation claim and not have to work for the rest of their lives. It was a viable alternative to Ed McMahon coming to their front door with a hand full of cash. Some even dubbed California worker's compensation as the "lifetime lottery."

Following the rush to file compensation injury claims, the '80s also saw the advent of the computer and other electronic devices in the workplace that had previously been used only sparingly, because of high cost and low availability. Such accessories as automatic voice mail, fax machines and computers had the effect of eliminating a lot of employees, so the question and issue of *com-*

mitment had do be dealt with. Many employees believed their jobs offered them a lifetime of employment, at least until they decided to retire. But layoffs due to automation and a reduced need for manpower changed all that. Suddenly, the question of the employer's commitment to the employee had to be explored.

Another factor was the large number of corporate takeovers, which led to such techniques as the isolation of unwanted employees (see discussion in chapter 8), summary terminations, reductions in benefits and salary adjustments. Because money and benefits are very emotional issues, by the mid-1990s emotions and their expression could no longer be kept under wraps or hidden. About that time, or just shortly before it, sexual harassment entered the picture. When this occurred, the cupboards and closets that disguised these issues were blown wide open, and leadership had to deal head on with the problems of sex, sexuality and emotion in the workplace. This was no easy task.

SEX, SEXUAL SURVIVAL AND THE ELEMENTS OF THE SEXUAL SURVIVAL MOTIVE

In chapter 3, the motives were introduced and examined in terms of their respective elements: emotions and benefits. We have carried out research in many product groups that have sexual identifications, such as fragrance, flowers, cowboy boots, guns, sporting ammunition, and the like. All of these are easily recognized as sexual *gender* items. Others are quickly identified as sexual *impulse* items, such as fast cars and fast boats, lingerie and beachwear. Still a third category of elements, not as easily recognized, consists of items that appeal to women's tendencies to be inhibited (sexual inhibition) or men's tendencies to be impotent (sexual impotence). Items in this category include a fragrance, *Jontue*, which makes the statement that it is "sensual . . . but not too far from innocence." Other products appealing to women's inhibition are the safe automobile and the "cover up" fashion or menswear that is made to be worn by women. The counterpart of inhibition in women is men who have problems with impotence, or failures in performance (not necessarily sexual). Products in this area include body-building kits and, more recently, a men's clinic franchise that offers relief from impotence and the ability to perform sexually for up to three hours simply by taking a shot.

These are the elements of the Sexual Survival Motive. Keep in mind that it is hard to understand the motives in and of themselves because they are abstract. The elements that are a part of each motive simply bring the motives down to earth and help us understand their functioning in everyday life.

SEXUAL GENDER

The element of sexual gender refers to the male/female issue in the Sexual Survival Motive. This was the first sexual issue to surface in the workplace, and it revolved around the controversy that started with the civil rights movement: equality. Equality for everyone was supposedly established with the Emancipation Proclamation, but in reality it did not come about until one hundred years later when President Lyndon Johnson announced the passage of the Civil Rights Bill of 1964. Still there was no real attempt to treat the races as equal until 1970, when schools began to integrate and the first companies to face federal compliance inspections—those that had government contracts—had to face the reality of inspections by federal compliance officers from the Equal Employment Opportunity Commission.

It was not long after that women began to feel they also had been discriminated against on the basis of *sexual gender*. Women began to seek protection under the aegis of the same agencies that had won substantial gains for African Americans—gains in employment, housing, education and other areas. At the workplace, men became confused. To a large degree, they did not realize there had been any discrimination. Suddenly, men and women became competitors for the same jobs. Although this is the way it should have been all along, the point here is that it merely intensified emotion and affect in the workplace. There was a lot of whispering going on—on both sides—and feelings of distrust and suspicion were intensified.

According to Farrell (1986), one of the problems was that men could not really understand what women wanted. Based on the magazine circulation statistics that were given in chapter 7, which updated Farrell's statistics from 1986, it would appear that what women wanted was marriage, security and children (not necessarily in that order). At least this was the message that men were getting at the time. So it was confusing when all of a sudden they came to work and were competing with women for their own positions. The confusion is to some extent understandable because the message men were getting from women was not that they wanted their jobs. As Farrell observed, "Over one hundred years ago, Freud asked the question, 'What do women really want?' This question is still without a clear answer, and the fear of being a male chauvinist has made them afraid to ask the questions necessary to get the answers" (p. xvii).

The fact that much of the gender issue cannot be openly discussed has caused an increase in hostility, anger and suspicion just below the surface, leaving the leader or manager in an even more precarious position. This is true regardless of whether the leader is male or female. And it is not that emotion cannot be dealt with, or even that feelings are more difficult to deal with. It is simply that managers and others have not been trained to deal with these issues. The reason they have not been trained is that there is no one to train them. Not only have we learned not to talk about emotion and feelings in business, but we have learned that it is dangerous to approach this subject. And so, there are all of the attempts at disguising emotion that were discussed in chapter 4.

At the heart of the gender issue in U.S. business and industry today is the fact that men and women are different, and they know it. Attempts to dress, act and think alike don't work for most men and women, and that's not what they want. Many are suspicious that a very small group of feminists who are also very vocal are calling the shots. Maybe so, and maybe not. But let's look at the issues strictly in terms of leadership.

GENDER AND LEADERSHIP ISSUES

The fact that men and women are different is one issue. It is not our place here to discuss these differences, other than to just give some examples. The literature is replete with articles and research that accentuate these differences. But let's look at just one striking example.

An area of considerable weakness for women is *direction*. When women are asked for directions they often become very confused and bewildered, saying "Don't ask me about north and west and that stuff. I don't understand it." When women come back from a cruise or a long trip, it is difficult for them to give the details of a trip in terms of distance or direction. On the other hand, stop any man and ask for directions and he acts as if he is delighted to oblige. In fact, most will stop whatever they are doing and often give directions in far too much detail.

On the other hand, an area of considerable weakness for men is *intuition*. Men have a much harder time than women spotting a phony, or knowing when another woman is showing an interest in them. They appear to overlook a lot of natural cues and body language to which women instinctively and intuitively attend. There are many more women than men who are psychics because psychics heavily rely on intuition. This is just one area where men and women differ substantially from one another.

There is an overabundance of research on gender differences in leadership, and most of this has just appeared since the late '80s. But we need to look at what these differences mean in terms of our own approach to leadership. Motivation is the key to leadership, and in order to deal with motivation one has to deal with emotion. This is not a voice in the wilderness. Many who have investigated transformational leaders and leadership have dealt with this same issue (Shamir, House and Arthur, 1993). It has been shown in chapters 2 and 4 that the activities of transformational leaders are a best fit with Fleischman's (1990) elements. The difference, however, is that Fleischman's approach deals directly with motivation, whereas Bass (1997) dealt with the issue of leadership, which is subsumed by motivation. If we are correct in saying that leadership is a subset of motivation and that leaders have to be motivators, then there is a good possibility that women will be more effective in leadership roles than men because of their expertise and experience dealing with human emotions. It is possible that those schooled in transformational leadership would agree with this. And if transformational (Bass, 1997) and motivational (Maddock and Fulton, 1996) approaches to leadership are on the horizon, as has been suggested here and elsewhere, then what does that say about women in leadership positions in the future?

What is important for our discussion is not who will be leading us into the next century, but what the implications are for the general direction of leadership theory. The major implication seen by us is that gender will become more important, and as it does, emotion will increasingly rise to the surface. Motivation will then not be an option as it is now; it will be dealt with directly and not indirectly. It is our projection also that many more women will secure leadership positions because of their effectiveness in dealing with emotions, because of some of the innate strengths they have such as intuition.

WHERE ARE THE WOMEN IN LEADERSHIP TODAY?

According to Weaver (1995), gender leaped into the picture with Tannen's book, *You Just Don't Understand*. More recently Gray's book, *Men Are From Mars, Women Are From Venus*, remained at the top of *The New York Times* best-seller list for one year. Any number of studies have been done on gender differences. Most of these studies have negligible or equivocal results and, like many research projects in the social sciences, raise more questions than they answer. According to the U.S. Department of Labor, in 1992 there was still a dearth of women at the executive levels in organizations, an observation that suggests that men have more leadership capability than women.

Typical of these studies is one conducted by Rosener (1990) that set the stage for many of the gender studies to follow. According to Rosener, in an article entitled "Ways Women Lead," there are substantial differences. Men lead by the traditional manner of "command and control." They give orders, reward with incentives and "keep their power and knowledge to themselves." Women lead in more nontraditional ways, by sharing information and power, inspiring good work by interacting with others, encouraging member participation and helping members relate personal goals to group goals. These findings are consistent with many of the studies conducted before and since that time. There are definite gender differences. Also these findings strongly suggest the major difference between men and women in their leadership styles is the same difference seen between transformational and transactional leadership styles: Women are more adaptable to a transformational leadership style, and men to a transactional "carrot on a stick" style.

However, a problem exists with many of these studies because they are based on "trait" theories of leadership, where women and men rate each other and themselves. In a study by Maher (1997), which was well controlled, she found no significant differences between men and women managers on transformational or transactional leadership. These findings are consistent with some of Bass' findings (1997), which suggest that gender differences between transformational and transactional leaders are far from universal. However, Maher did find a significant interaction effect that indicated that women view other women as more transformational. She concluded that if this finding holds up, women who are now in power may select other women into leadership in organizations, "particularly if transformational leaders are called upon more and more to guide organizations through change" (p. 224).

The problem with the ratings and with rating scales being used in many of these studies is that they do not control for the inherent bias that exists between men and women. For example, it is conceded that Farrell's (1986) observations were not made under conditions of rigorous scientific control. Nevertheless, there is something to be said for the value of ethnographic research because it is not as rigorous but is much broader in scope. From his observations, Farrell concluded that the primary need in a man, when looking at a woman, was beauty. If this observation is at all accurate, then even the untrained person can see the problem inherent in men rating women for leadership styles and abilities. There is an immediate confound present that biases the results.

SEXUAL IMPULSE

For well-known and well-established reasons, the Sexual Survival Motive always causes trouble and confusion wherever it is encountered: in advertising, in the workplace and even at home. But like the other Survival Motives, it is essential and fundamental. It has to be reckoned with rather than tucked under the carpet and ignored. This is especially true of the sexual impulse element of sex and sexuality because whenever the Sexual Survival Motive causes trouble, it will be brought on by impulse. Impulse relates to the sex drive itself.

In 1966, Ford advertised the new Mustang by saying "We made it hot, you make it scream." That is impulse, and it is also what started Ralph Nader on his lifelong career as a crusader for consumer rights.

A restauranteur whom we interviewed in one of our studies said he always put a beautiful woman behind the dessert cart because he knew that dessert was strictly an impulse item and as such, would only be purchased by men. This strategy worked very well for him.

In 1952, when Chrysler was struggling for its existence, Ernst Dichter, the psychologist-gadfly-consultant, convinced Chrysler to put the convertible on the floor to bring the men in, and then their wives or girlfriends would make the "intelligent" decision. That's impulse.

This is not to imply that women don't have impulses. Women, however, are more subtle and more controlled. So until lately, most products sold on the basis of impulse have gone to men.

In business and other leadership situations, sexual impulse has been ignored and overlooked. Of all the emotions discussed here, this one can be the ugliest, the hardest to deal with and the one that is veiled in the most secrecy. But this secrecy was blasted away in organizations when the issue of sexual harassment was brought to the surface in the mid-'90s.

With the advent of sexual harassment charges it was no longer possible to hide emotion in the workplace. And with sexual harassment, what is being dealt with is real, true hard-core emotion. The kind that embarrasses everyone.

Unlike gender confusion and discrimination, sexual harassment is very hard to prove. Most of the cases have involved anecdotal evidence rather than real, hard evidence. Extreme confusion comes into the picture when those who are in charge of enforcement are themselves involved in sexual harassment. Like cancer or other diseases, sexual harassment is no respecter of persons. It can attack anyone, at any time.

HOW TO AVOID SEXUAL HARASSMENT CHARGES

The organization that has effective leadership does not have sexual harassment charges. The reason has been expressed in several of the foregoing chapters: The building blocks of the pyramid are in order. The effective leader does not allow the building blocks to become disordered or disarranged in the hierarchy. That's why there are rules and regulations in almost every organization about sex, sexual activity and sexual acting-out in the workplace.

But it takes more than rules. It requires a lot of common sense. For example, we are told by some that we are moving closer to a "genderless society." In a genderless society, men and women travel together for business necessity and they often live together on warships and in college dormitories. But sexual impulse is still a factor. We may live (as we are told) in a genderless society, but we still must reckon with sexual *impulse*. The U.S. Navy learned this when it put men and women together on a carrier. When the ship returned, Navy spokespeople conceded there were five pregnancies. Later this count was revised upward and at final count twenty-nine pregnancies were reported. Business organizations learn this when men and women travel together and eventually run off with each other, leaving their families of origin behind.

The effective leader is aware not only of sex in the workplace, but is keenly aware of the three aspects of the Sexual Survival Motive: gender, impulse and inhibition. At times this will create a very difficult and confusing situation. For example, in order to ensure that women as well as men have equality in the workplace, women have an equal opportunity to apply for jobs involving travel. But despite how rational, logical and responsible we may think we are, we cannot ignore impulse. Impulse is biological. Impulse is also an emotion. As a biological urge and an emotion, impulse is much stronger than logic, common sense or judgment.

Sexual harassment charges are avoided by keeping the building blocks of the pyramid in the proper order and sequence. Although this may differ from one location to another and from one business to another, the building blocks are essentially the same. For example, consider the confusion that exists between sex and love.

CONFUSION BETWEEN SEX AND LOVE

Generally when two individuals at work begin to have an affair, in defiance of the rules and regulations of the organization, they will continue the affair and justify it on the basis of the fact that they are in love with each other. Then, when caught, they will justify it to their supervisor on the same basis: They are in love.

Here is an excellent example of shifting the blocks around in the structure of human motivation for reasons that are self-serving. What appears to be—and what is—sexual impulse has been elevated by them to the category of spiritual survival. This is because they say they are in love, and love, as you may remember, is one of the vital elements of spiritual survival as defined by Fleischman and described in chapter 4. They elevate sexual impulse to the category of love and spiritual survival, not only because they want to justify their behavior to management, but also because they believe it to be true themselves. This is why it is so difficult to break up relationships like this: The people themselves believe they are "in love." Management and leadership thus have only one choice: The building blocks of the pyramid have to be put back into the proper order, or the individuals involved have to be terminated. One way to put the blocks back in order is to help the individuals see the difference between sexual survival (impulse) and love (spiritual survival). This gives the leader a framework or a paradigm to work within.

It was mentioned earlier that women often make better leaders than men, and some of the research that looks at this issue was reviewed. However, we look at it here in an entirely different light. The issue between gender–impulse–inhibition is more effectively dealt with by women than by men because of the innate ability that women have to rely on their intuition. Many women can see the attraction developing between a man and a woman long before it becomes common knowledge. Furthermore, many women—not all— can *address* this situation more effectively and more directly than a man. This is the focus of this whole approach to leadership, which is a *motivational approach.* And motivation is emotion.

SEXUAL INHIBITION

The third element of sexual survival is *sexual inhibition.*

Inhibition is a gender-specific term. There are no inhibited men, or at least we never associate the term with men—only with women. But a closely equivalent term that is associated with men is *impotence.* This is a term that is rarely if ever associated with women. The two terms are not identical in meaning, but close. Because the history of our culture involves avoidance of discussions on sex and sexual issues, there is somewhat of a deficit of terms and terminology in sexual language. This is because, as linguists tell us, culture determines language.

A sexually inhibited woman is generally considered a person who does not enjoy performing, sexually. An impotent man is generally considered an individual who cannot perform sexually, either permanently or temporarily.

Sexual inhibition is entirely appropriate in the workplace. The prescribed clothing or "uniform of the day" for both men and women plays down or minimizes the role of emotion and sexuality. According to Farrell (1986), women's clothing in particular is designed to be appealing to men, and men are in turn interested in women who are attractive and "pretty." Therefore, if women wear attractive seductive clothing to work, it might attract men's attention and create problems with the sexual impulse element. This is why there is a prescribed manner for the way men and women should dress and for their overall appearance at work. Sexual inhibition is a key emotional element in the workplace.

According to Ashworth, who quoted Hatfield, Cacioppo and Rapson (1992), there is an emotional contagion in the workplace, which they defined as "a tendency to mimic another person's emotional experience/expression . . . and thus to experience/express the same emotions oneself" (p. 151). In other words, people will "catch" the prevailing emotional or affective "wave" in much the same way they will catch a cold. If a high-status team leader is optimistic, outgoing and cheerful, this mood will permeate the workplace. However—and this is our whole thesis—that same type of overwhelming optimism could also have a very strong *destructive* effect on performance if that optimism and cheerfulness get out of control.

For example: In a factory that assembled furniture for bottom-of-the-line furniture stores, cabinets and chests-of-drawers were assembled with stapling guns. Ten employees worked in this area of the plant. They were not closely supervised and had time for "fun and games." However, this playful feeling quickly led to hostility and oppositional behavior, and eventually resulted in minor injuries as employees shot at each other with the stapling guns that were used to fasten together the furniture frames, increasing hostility and aggression to perform the same volume of work. As a result, the company installed computerized fitting and stapling jigs, which required only two people instead of ten.

This kind of behavior is consistent with observations of a medical subsidiary that found that, through neglect by the parent company, negative feelings led to atrophy, apathy, depression and despondency and a considerable decrease in productivity.

The role of the company party has many opponents as well as proponents, and the proponents generally promote it as a once-a-year affair to "maintain company morale." However, opponents resist it because this once-a-year affair can easily turn into a once-a-month affair, quickly giving employees the wrong opinion of the nature of their work. Furthermore, when company gatherings involve drinking, which changes the emotional status of many participants as soon as they take the first drink, the result is often disastrous. Many companies have completely discontinued any gatherings involving alcohol consumption because recent changes in insurance regulations and coverage assigns responsibility to the premises where the drinks were served for any injuries that occur afterward.

CONCLUSION

Motivation is the outgrowth of emotion. Emotions exist in both personal and group situations. Emotions cannot be eliminated. The effective leader deals with emotion because he or she is a motivator. Nowhere is this more apparent than in dealing with the Sexual Survival Motive.

Sex cannot be eliminated in the workplace, but it can be controlled. And it is controlled, not by waiting until sexual situations erupt and break through to the surface, but by making certain on the front end that all of the building blocks of the structure of human motivation are in place. It is easier to put these pieces in place on the front end and to maintain them than it is to "pick up the pieces" after the fact.

REFERENCES

Ashworth, B. E. (1995). Emotion in the workplace: A reappraisal. *Human Relations 48*(2), 97.

Bass, B. M. (1997). Does the transactional-transformational leadership paradigm transcend organizational boundaries? *American Psychologist 52*(2), 130–139.

Farrell, W. (1986). *Why men are the way they are.* New York: McGraw-Hill.

Fleischman, P. (1990). *The healing spirit.* New York: Paragon House.

Hatfield, E., Cacioppo, J., & Rapson, R. L. (1992). Primitive emotional contagion. In M. S. Clark (Ed.), *Review of personality and social psychology* (Vol. 14, pp. 151–177). Newbury Park, CA: Sage Books.

Maddock, R. C., & Fulton, R. L. (1996). *Marketing to the mind: Right brain strategies in advertising and marketing.* Westport, CT: Quorum Books.

Maher, K. J. (1997). Gender-related stereotypes of transformational and transactional leadership. *Sex Roles 37*(3/4), 209–225.

Rosener, J. (1990, November). Ways women lead. *Harvard Business Review*, p. 68.

Shamir, B., House, R. J., & Arthur, M. B. (1993). The motivational effect of charismatic leadership: A self-concept based theory. *Organizational Science 4*, 577–594.

Weaver, R. L. (1995, May). Leadership for the future: A new set of priorities. *Vital Speeches 61*(14) 438–441.

Chapter 12

Place Orientation and Leadership

WHAT DOES IT MEAN TO BE ORIENTED TO PLACE?

The classic meaning of place orientation in the psychiatric mental status test was knowing where one was at the time, and how one got there and what to do to get out in the event of an emergency. This is an essential part of the test that is used in discerning whether an elderly person should be admitted to a nursing home.

Wherever you happen to be, there are certain kinds of demands placed on you by the environment you are in. If you are a visitor in a hospital, you are expected to be quiet, courteous and exhibit appropriate behavior by remaining in the areas marked for visitors and not wandering off into operating suites, the recovery room or intensive care. If you are a student at school, you are expected to attend classes with regularity, listen, take notes and be prepared for a test when one is given. In addition, if the teacher assigns homework you are expected to do it. If you work in an industrial or business organization, you are expected to be on time, know your job and your job description and be able to produce your reasonable quotas. If you are in sales, you are expected to meet your sales quotas and when not selling to behave appropriately, particularly if you are in someone else's place of business. Almost anywhere you go there are expectations, guidelines and procedures that have to be followed; even in your own home.

EXAMPLE 1: PLACE ORIENTATION IN A LARGE PUBLIC SCHOOL SYSTEM

This is all very simple and straightforward. And yet this block can get out of place in the pyramid and cause major problems, as in the following example.

A very large urban high school in a large city prided itself on its records in football and basketball, but particularly in basketball. Indeed, this particular school was responsible for sending a number of players to prestigious colleges and universities in the SEC, the Big Ten and other highly competitive associations. Their record was impeccable, and each year they would go to the state championship and would often return with first, second or third place trophies. An investigative reporter began to ask questions and wrote down the responses on his pad. What he was hearing was to him, at that time, unbelievable. The school was engaged in major recruiting efforts, some of them even in a neighboring state. Most of the recruits came from the urban area outside the school's location, but their parents were paid to move into the school's district so their son could be eligible to play basketball in that school. Large sums of money had been withdrawn from the athletic account and were unaccounted for. There was even suspicion that some of this had gone for "gifts" that would entice players and their families to move to the district. Furthermore, and after an extended investigation of this issue, it was revealed that (a) some of the players were attending school with regularity only during the basketball season; (b) special arrangements had been made to place players in special education classes so they would always remain eligible to play; and (c) there were some isolated incidents in which players' parents were offered jobs within the school cafeteria, or as janitors, secretaries and teachers' aides. After further investigation, it was found that this was not the only school with such an aggressive sports recruiting program, but in fact every high school in the system had an identical recruiting program!

Why does this offend us? Why, in a city that loves basketball and loves even more to see its team win does this strike a discord? Is this a problem in leadership? In motivation? In greed or in pride? What is the problem?

Let's look at it from the vantage point of the Place Orientation Motive. A school is a place set aside for learning and particularly for providing people with education and skills to cope with the future. But that was not the case at this school, nor with any of the other schools in the system that engaged in the same practices. For the principal and assistant principal, the teachers and on down to the custodians, this school was a place to train and coach promising athletes and to produce winning teams. Teachers who did not cooperate by assigning grades that would afford their students eligibility were quickly transferred to another school, usually to one in which there was no sports program and that was in an undesirable location.

When all of this information surfaced, thirteen top administrators and teachers lost their jobs, having been sacrificed so the school system could save face. The problem was caused by shifting the blocks in the pyramid of human motivation from lower to higher positions. Also, there was a large number of people who were disoriented to place. They had come to believe, for one reason or another, that the education part of the school was secondary, and that the sports program was primary.

How Do the Building Blocks of Motivation Get Misplaced?

This is the same situation seen in chapter 4. In all of these schools, basketball specifically and sports in general had been moved from a position of play to a position of territorial survival, and eventually into a position of spiritual survival. The coaches and officials in the schools with their records of many wins and few losses began living in a surrealistic world (see chapter 4). The primary characteristic of surrealism, as in surrealistic art and paintings, is that the boundaries fade and are often indistinguishable. Just like the example of Coach Switzer walking through the airport gate with a loaded gun, these coaches and administrators felt they were due the same privileges. Their records were impressive; the crowds were even more impressive and the gate receipts would make a small college sit up and take notice.

The situation presented here went too far to be resolved by ordinary, less drastic methods, short of everyone losing their jobs. But this is not simply because no one was watching the chicken coop. If they had been watching, they would not have known what to look for. However, if they had a graphic of the pyramid of human motivation clearly fixed in their mind's eyes, they would have seen the building blocks gradually slipping out of position, and the ones that were less vital becoming more and more vital. In this case, vital refers to the school's primary mission: the education of students and their preparation for the future. This is in contrast to the school putting almost all of its resources into preparing athletes for the NBA.

Some would explain the occurrence of this problem as a problem with the character of the leaders: the coaches, administrators and teachers in the schools involved (e.g., Barone, 1995; Crouse, 1994;

Plummer, 1995). They would say it is a problem with the integrity, honesty and substance of the involved adults. But surely not all of these people could have been of doubtful character. After all, schools have to screen their personnel very carefully and advertently. They cannot afford to be careless. Perhaps some of those involved were of doubtful character and integrity, but surely that was not true of all. For this reason, we feel that inattention to motives and motivation is a much better explanation, and a more encompassing explanation is that they just did not know what motivates people, and how they are motivated. They looked out over this large sea of faces on game night, and then counted the receipts the next day, and felt they had a real handle on motivation. But as it turned out, they didn't.

Orientation to place. This is a motive that accounts for a lot of losses and upsets. But when you learn it is a motive and that it has its rightful position in the pyramid of human motivation, accidents are much less likely to occur.

EXAMPLE 2: PLACE ORIENTATION IN HEALTH CARE

Hospitals have an obligation to treat patients for their illnesses and injuries. For most people, this is what health care is all about. Either a hospital has an obligation to cure the patient or, if that is impossible, to treat the patient to the best of its ability and then allow the patient to spend his or her final days in dignity and self-respect. This is what most people think of when they think of a health care facility, and particularly a hospital.

But hospitals have a secondary responsibility: to train residents and interns in medicine, and all of its various specialties and sub-specialties. This activity is expensive, and requires an investment in equipment that typically runs in the millions of dollars. To purchase and sustain this equipment, large margins are required that can come only from patient revenue. Because the hospitals with the best and most updated equipment always get the best residents, this secondary activity—training residents—becomes a hotly contested, dog-eat-dog battle in which large and small hospitals are pitted against each other in what has become a battle for survival.

Expensive equipment, whether it is purchased for patient treatment or for the purpose of attracting residents, is part of a hospital's obligation. However, when that expensive equipment is duplicated by nine hospitals within a sixty-square-block area in a large medical center, it begins to border on the absurd. Expensive CAT scanning and MRI equipment can sit unused for days at a time. But even if it is unused, the principal and the interest payments come due each month and someone has to write the checks. The alternative is to share with other hospitals in the same area. But because of the competitive nature of health care today, this alternative is not often seen as viable.

What are the other alternatives? First the hospital can pressure physicians to make more extensive use of the equipment and to order more tests and screenings. This pressure is often applied, but in a subtle and not obvious manner. In the last ten to twelve years, since the introduction of diagnostic related groups (in which patients are restricted to the number of days they can remain in the hospital in accordance with their diagnosis), a hospital or health care organization might be more likely to do this. Other alternatives include downsizing, reducing health care research, cutting corners in employee benefits and forming conglomerates. Some hospitals, in their confusion, even go so far as to inflate their billings, particularly to Medicare and Medicaid, with the assumption that they will never be caught. Billing for tests and procedures that never took place is not common, but it does occur in places where it might least be suspected.

The confusion over the actual role of the hospital—between treating patients and training new doctors—is clearly a confusion in orientation to place. Just what is the role of the hospital? Or if it has a dual role, how is it best handled for the benefit of all who are concerned, doctors and patients considered? The enlightened leader looks at the pyramid and then makes his or her moves to put the blocks back in the proper order. This is the simplest, most parsimonious and most effective solution.

EXAMPLE 3: TIME AND PLACE ORIENTATION IN HEALTH CARE

By now you should be familiar with how the motives in the pyramid of human motivation interfere with the smooth and efficient operation of schools, hospitals and other organizations having a primary purpose. This makes it look as if the leader's job is usually to help subordinates reorder priorities. But a second and even more important part of the leader's job description is to make sure the motives never get out of place again. The key to keeping them in place is constant and continual monitoring.

Now that some examples have been given relating primarily to a conflict in one motivational block, we look at one that involves a conflict between two motivational blocks in the pyramid. Such a conflict often occurs.

A sixteen-year-old male experienced acute pain in the lower abdominal quadrant that was quickly recognized by his parents as appendicitis. It was Christmas Eve. He was quickly taken to a local hospital, a laproscopic procedure was performed and he was sent to recovery. His parents waited in the surgical waiting room for him to be brought up from surgery, since they were told that it would be about one hour. After ninety minutes, they began to be concerned, and in one hour and forty-five minutes they asked the nurse to call recovery. She did, and was told that he was ready and would be right up. When he did come, the boy's mother quickly recognized that something was wrong. His color, his temperature and other signs did not appear to her to be right. She asked the nurse to take vital signs and they were found to be extremely low. After some attempts to improve the patient's condition, a physician was called in from the emergency room. He quickly mobilized a team to return the boy to the operating room and perform surgery immediately, on what he diagnosed as internal bleeding. In his estimation, an artery had been inadvertently clipped during the laproscopic procedure and the patient was losing blood. His blood pressure was down to 25/12. This was a real emergency.

A second surgery was performed and one week later a third, to straighten out a twisted intestine that occurred during the second surgery. A subsequent investigation uncovered no negligence on the part of the surgeon, but gross negligence on the part of the recovery room team who were engaged in having a Christmas party in the office at the time this patient was in recovery. Because all of the team knew ahead of time that they would be working on Christmas Eve, the party had been planned several weeks in advance. One of the technicians was detailed to draw up a list that told each employee what food items he or she should bring to the party.

This is a clear-cut conflict between time orientation (a major holiday) and place orientation (the function of a hospital is not to sponsor parties and gala events). Some would probably agree with these employees that they were entitled to have a party on Christmas Eve at their work stations, because the hospital census is notoriously very low on Christmas Eve and there is very little to do. Furthermore, Christmas is a special time of the year and it only comes around once a year.

But this kind of reasoning ignores the position of two of the crucial blocks in the pyramid: the time orientation block and the place orientation block. These employees were all being paid double time for their willingness to work on Christmas Eve. Some had even volunteered because of the extra holiday pay they would receive. Furthermore, they were working in a critical situation and with only one patient, whom they virtually ignored. The fact that the on-board party had been planned weeks in advance indicates that they probably had very little or possibly no intention of working that night, because it was Christmas Eve. So we repeat, a hospital is a place to treat and cure patients (place orientation) and Christmas is a time to relax and party (time orientation), but not if you are being paid overtime to care for sick people and are placed in a position of heavy responsibility: saving lives.

Although hospital staff are generally tuned in to having parties for just about any occasion, it is probably not a good idea. In fact, it is a bad idea. Place orientation in this situation tells us that a hospital is not a place to party; it is a place for sick people to get well. The effective leader would risk his or her popularity with employees in this case and put the blocks of the pyramid back in order again.

The patient lived, but only because of the heroic efforts of some nurses and doctors who thought quickly and moved to save his life. No one should die from a routine appendectomy, and they should not even come as close to death as this young boy did.

Where was leadership? The pyramid of human motivation would tell us that they were probably celebrating Christmas Eve also, at home, with their families. But that's okay, because the fix should have come long before this incident occurred. Who would have ever recognized that a simple Christmas party would have caused major motivational problems? But then again, who would have ever recognized that a simple Christmas party would have almost taken the life of a young man who had been headed down a road of success and brilliance in academics, in athletics and in life?

REFERENCES

Barone, M. (1995). Bill, meet Niccolo: Bill Clinton's approach to leadership is the opposite of Prince Niccolo Machiavelli's. *U.S. News and World Report 119*(11), 59.

Crouse, J. S. (1994). Leadership: Working from the inside out. *Vital Speeches 60*(19), 597.

Plummer, L. C. (1995). In pursuit of honest leadership. *FBI Law Enforcement Bulletin 64*(4), 16.

Chapter 13

Time Orientation and Leadership

ESCAPING FROM THE RESTRAINTS OF TIME

Time orientation is that sense we all possess of the approximate date and hour. It is not nearly so strong as personal and place orientation. Accordingly, when we become engrossed in some interesting activity, we lose track of time. Likewise, after a dream in which past and present have been blurred, time orientation is sometimes confused. Among elderly people, time orientation can be severely, permanently destroyed as brain deterioration damages the internal clock.

But time is a constraint we all like to escape now and then. In fact, the fun of doing so has generated whole industries: theme parks, resorts and restaurants whose settings create the feel of past or future times.

Some elements of time orientation include urgency, timing, rhythm and beat. Most of us also have an internal alarm clock that wakes us up at a certain time and also tells us when we are hungry, thirsty, and so on. An individual who never drinks during the week but enjoys happy hour on Friday evening after work will begin to taste the scotch rolling across his or her tongue as the bewitching hour approaches, perhaps even before leaving work that day.

We continually and aggressively battle against the restraints of time. At work and at school, getting people to come in on time is a never-ending battle. Tardiness and absenteeism are common enemies that have to be fought almost daily by school principals and plant managers. This is evidence, if not proof, that many people resist the constraints of time and say, silently, "I won't let this clock dictate to me and the way I run my life."

But there are also managers who have to fight to get their employees to go home at night. This is particularly true in one industry: software development. One manager told us that he had to beg his employees to go home, and then when they did, they would stay up another five hours, working on the same project. He asked, "What in the world motivates them?"

We see the same kind of attentiveness in children who play computer and video games. Children who can barely sit still—children with hyperactivity or attention deficit disorder—can play video games for hours on end. Doesn't this appear as a paradox? Teachers complain and tell parents their children cannot remain still or quiet for more than two or three minutes, and yet the parents have watched them play video games for up to four hours. Is this a paradox, or is there an explanation?

DISORIENTATION TO TIME AS A STATE OF HYPNOSIS

When a person engages in an activity that disengages or disconnects him or her from that ongoing, eternal ticking clock, it is similar, if not identical to hypnosis, meditation or deep relaxation. And the state itself includes relaxation. This is the reason why *disorientation to time* is so relaxing and peaceful, and therefore motivating. Many activities in which people engage are designed to disorient from time. We have already mentioned casinos and how they are set up so they disorient in all four spheres: person, place, time and circumstance. Time in particular is carefully attended to by management by making certain that there are no visible clocks, no windows and no entryways that allow someone to see the outside from where the main gaming room is located. We have interviewed women who sew, and although there are not many left, the ones that still do it tell us they lose complete track of time when sewing. Computers are also a way we can disconnect from time, and particularly with the Internet with its seemingly infinite number of links. Almost any hobby that absorbs an individual's interest will effectively remove him or her from time, and normally that is at least 50 percent of the purpose of the hobby.

DISORIENTATION TO TIME IS ADDICTIVE

Although most of the activities that help us to disorient to time are not chemically dangerous or addictive, they can become addictive in their own right. This is also true of thrill seeking and of gambling, as well as some other more strenuous activities such as mountain climbing, surfboarding, bungee jumping and parachuting. Just because they are not chemical does not mean that they are not addictive. Zuckerman (1986) believes that the fear stimulated by these activities causes an alteration in the level of monoamine oxidase, which changes the thrill seeker's mood.

Farley (1986) says that thrill seekers and others who regularly seek disorientation often act as if they are addicted, and it is very possible that the opioid receptors of the brain are involved. Farley thinks that these people have a low arousal level and the feeling of being in danger triggers the reticular activating system in the brain, which in turn stimulates other neuromodulators and neurotransmitters in the rest of the brain. If the opioid receptors are part of this chain, then addiction among thrill seekers as well as others who are regularly seeking disorientation may be more easily understood. Consider the illustrations that were just given above regarding casinos. If one of the major attractions of the casino is disorientation in all four spheres, which they are quite good at, then isn't it more understandable how many gamblers become addicted? Are they really addicted to gambling, or just to disorientation? Or what about the compulsive shoppers who buy everything that they see on the Value Channel, or the depressed woman who goes out and buys new clothing?

Henry Ford once gave his explanation for going into the automobile business. He said "Everybody wants to get where they ain't, and then when they get there they want to get back home again." Even running away can become addictive and compulsive, because of the effect that it has on each individual, and upon the neurotransmitters of the central nervous system.

IT'S ONLY A MATTER OF TIME

A medium-sized manufacturing company was experiencing great difficulty in maintaining an executive's performance at one location. Although there were many problems, all seemed to come from the style of a general manager. It was learned that the general manager was an experienced manager prior to assuming the top spot. Likewise he was technically competent. He knew a lot about the business. Indeed he had served as department manager in several departments prior to assuming the general manager role. He knew a lot of detail about the intricacy of the operation, even though he had never served at the level of general manager. He was almost "too knowledgeable" technically, although he was not the typical "technician micro-manager."

The problem was that, even though the general manager was technically competent, seasoned, and the promotion did not go to his head, he seemed to thrive on the verbal and nonverbal support that he received from his supervisor, who was a regional vice president of the company. He looked forward to the daily conversations that they had with each other in the initial stages of his tenure as general manager. But it didn't stop there. Soon the daily conversation was extended into weekends and evenings. He would call his supervisor two, three and four times a day to apprise him of trivial situations, and to seek guidelines as well as support. His calls would typically last thirty to forty-five minutes, and if three or four times a day didn't do it, he would then call the supervisor at home. Eventually, some of these calls would last an hour, and some of them two hours. Weekends were not sacred, as he would call on Saturdays and Sundays. If unable to reach the supervisor, he would become more insistent and call back several times, leaving the message that "I must talk with him."

Interestingly neither the general manager nor his supervisor ever dealt with the issue of time. We'll see why in just a moment. For the general manager, time was of no importance. He had no family, no obligations outside of work, and he worked seven days a week and twelve to fourteen hours a day. He had no outside interests such as sports or hobbies. Conversely, for his supervisor time was extremely important and very limited. He managed three other plants and regularly had to go to meetings at corporate headquarters for planning purposes. And the general manager not only tied up his supervisor for hours at a time but, as you have probably already guessed, it was impossible for him to have a "brief" meeting with any of his subordinates. Any issue, no matter how trivial, even if it involved emptying the ashtrays in the break room after they were used, took at least thirty minutes and often an hour.

Since the general manager had no concept of time, he was eventually discharged. And this is tragic, since he was a good, motivated and hard working, technically competent employee. But no one every talked to him about his problem. Instead, they just terminated him. Why?

The reason that no one ever talked to him is that time orientation is an emotion, and no one wants to bring emotions into the workplace. Managers and particularly senior managers will avoid emotion at all costs. When it comes to terminating someone or to a necessary confrontation, no matter how small it is, everyone attempts to avoid it. In this case, the supervisor was just as much to blame as the general manager. In the end, the general manager lost his job and the company lost a good and competent employee.

You have probably never thought about time orientation as a motive or an emotion, but it is. Just the fact that it is shunned as a topic shows that it is treated in the same way that the topic of sex would be treated. And if you think that this is an isolated incident, think again.

WHO'S GOT THE MONKEY?

An article in the *Harvard Business Review*, which is now considered a classic, entitled "Who's got the monkey?" (Oncken and Wass, 1974), indicates that one of the biggest problems that a manager has is time, and the reason is because of the failure to manage it properly. The authors characterize the everyday problems that arise as monkeys. In the hour-to-hour and day-to-day schedule of a manager, he is greeted by at least ten or twelve subordinates a day who say "oh by the way, we have a problem over in transportation" or "we have a problem in product returns." Each problem is a monkey, and in the transaction between the subordinate and the manager that monkey is transferred from the subordinate's back to the manager's back and guess who ends up with all the monkeys? As a result the manager has no time left, and all of the subordinates have freed themselves up for golf games on Saturday and Sunday.

Why does the manager end up with all of the monkeys? Simply because he won't talk to his subordinates about time. Time is emotional, and therefore time is an emotional issue. Rather than deal with it straight on, and in a forward, upright manner, the manager would rather stack all the monkeys on his desk, even at the risk of losing his weekend and any other time that he might have left over from his busy schedule. Even that is preferred over having to deal in a straightforward way about the issue of time with his subordinates.

HOW TO DEAL CONSTRUCTIVELY WITH THE EMOTIONAL ISSUE OF TIME ORIENTATION

There is a very constructive and simple way to deal with the emotional and motivational issue of time orientation. All that needs to be said by the manager when he feels that his time is being monopolized and not respected, is that he is very short on time today, and can spend only a few minutes on whatever the subject is. This statement imparts a sense of urgency to the subordinate and as you recall, urgency is one of the elements of time orientation. In most cases, when given this simple statement, subordinates will say whatever they have to say and then get up out of the chair and leave, simply because they have been placed under and feel the conditions of urgency.

In the case of the supervisor discussed earlier, he complained bitterly to everyone about how the general manager was monopolizing his time and how he resented it. But he never said anything to the general manager directly, and never made any attempt to correct it. For the same reason: time orientation is an emotional issue. It would have been very simple to explain to the general manager about the time constraints that he was under, not only with heavy responsibilities but also because of the demands of his own family. But he never did. Therefore he was just as responsible for encouraging this situation as the general manager was for initiating it.

TIME'S UP!

In every train-the-trainer or public speaking class, a segment of the training devotes itself to the mechanics of time. Students are instructed to time the various segments of a speech, verbal report or session and then to stick to the time allotments. In addition, students are told to set the stage for those segments by referring to them in an agenda, or if no agenda is set, by starting the talk by specifically stating the time that the talk will take. This is the single most important component of public speaking.

The point is that we all have an internal clock, and we all stay oriented to time, unless we intentionally disorient to time. Going over the allotted time can render the most dazzling speech to the "over and forgotten basket" just as surely as a poorly written or poorly delivered speech. This is because of the power of the Time Orientation Motive. People order their lives in terms of little segments that are measured by time. A violation of this motive disrupts these elements and the emotions involved.

Time is a significant motivator because it determines to a large extent what we remember and what we don't remember. The reason that Bill Clinton was even considered for president in 1992 is that four years before, he had read a prepared speech that placed the nomination of Michael Dukakis before the Democratic party for President. The speech was not written by him, and it was long, dreary and repetitious. It was so long and redundant that no one forgot it. As a result of this lengthy and dreary speech Bill Clinton had no choice but to laugh about it and joke about it, and for the next four years he appeared on talk shows and on radio stations, talking about his speech which had become famous. And four years later, people still remembered. And that's how he became President of the United States!

REFERENCES

Farley, F. (1986). The big T in personality. *Psychology Today 20*, 44–52.
Oncken, W., & Wass, D. L. (1974, November–December). Who's got the monkey? *Harvard Business Review.*
Zuckerman, M. (1986). Sensation seeking and the endogenous deficit theory of drug abuse. In the *Research Monograph Series* (Monograph No. 74, pp. 59–70). Rockville, MD: National Institute on Drug Abuse.

Chapter 14

Circumstances Orientation and Leadership

HAPPY HOUR

The Circumstances Orientation Motive is the weakest of all of the motives in the pyramid because it is short-lived. At the time that circumstances occur, they can be overwhelming and overpowering; but they usually don't last that long. Whatever the circumstances on any particular day and at any time of the day, they can usually be overcome or knocked out with a drink or two. In other words, the simplest of all the motivations to disconnect or disorient from is the Circumstances Orientation Motive. This is what people mean when they say "I've got to unwind. Let's go to happy hour."

Happy hour is so named because it comes at the end of the day, allowing an escape from the circumstances of the day. If happy hour was moved to breakfast time it would be disastrous because that is the time of day that we face and anticipate the circumstances. There are, however, some people who do have happy hour at breakfast time, and this is an example of taking *disorientation* and carrying it too far. With any of the motives discussed in this book, there are two ever present dangers for the leader. The first is misplacing the motives in the pyramid of human motivation. The second is going too far with disorientation–disconnection–escape. Either of these two conditions will cause problems for leadership and call for intervention and immediate remedies on the part of the leader. Having happy hour at breakfast time is an example of the second danger: going too far with disorientation.

Although we all have some control over circumstances, we do not have complete control. Downsizing, illness, business reversals—all of these things may strike at any time, and we know that. The answer is never to run away. Temporary disorientation, disconnection and evasion are usually appropriate, but sooner or later circumstances have to be dealt with.

THE ELEMENTS OF CIRCUMSTANCES

The elements of circumstances, as seen in Table 3.2, are convenience and pace.

Convenience refers to the road of least resistance. When we conduct studies with consumers and ask them why they bank at Bank XYZ or shop at ABC Supermarket, they usually respond "It's convenient." Convenience is a motivator, and is part of the Circumstances Orientation Motive. Compare, for example, convenience shopping with pleasure shopping. Two women who spend one Thursday afternoon each month shopping for antiques don't mind driving one hundred miles to get to that certain antique dealer who has exactly what they want, or think they want. These same two women would never even think of moving to a home where the nearest grocery store was fifteen miles away. In the same vein, we might drive twenty-five or thirty miles to get to a restaurant we enjoy, passing fifteen or twenty other restaurants along the way. But when we get home at 7 P.M. and haven't had time to prepare dinner, the closest fast food restaurant will do.

The second major element of the Circumstances Orientation Motive is *pace*, which refers to the pace of life. At any time of day and in almost any place, you can drop in on a conversation that refers to the pace of life. This was not true ten or fifteen years ago, but it is today. Computers, electronics, microchips and networks have changed our pace of life. There is no way that the human brain can keep up with the speed of a computer. And now that we no longer can keep up, the pace of life is threatening to smother us as we run faster and faster to keep up. Pace is a big issue—all day, every day. In fact, this issue came out in the factor analysis we did on Fleischman's (1990) elements of spiritual survival, and can be seen in Table 5.2. We did not intend for it to come out, but it did. It was the fourth factor that emerged. We do not consider it to be a viable part of the Spiritual Survival Motive, but perhaps it is. This whole issue will take more study and research.

There are certain kinds of activities that require a disorientation from pace. We once did a study for a bank that had installed small "mini" banks in supermarket stores. They did very well because they were one of the first banks to pursue this concept. However, they wondered why people did not do *serious* banking in supermarket banks. They didn't finance cars or houses, take out second mortgages or start businesses. The reason was simple: Supermarket banks were in the fast lane. No one wants to do serious banking in the fast lane. Cash registers were ringing, people were shouting and supermarket carriages were being shoved together by bag boys. Imagine trying to balance your checkbook amidst that kind of chaos! Supermarket banking. Convenient? Yes. But what about the pace? It is overwhelming. Many people told us that if they intended to do *real banking* that they would go to a *real bank*.

Sometimes, convenience and pace are in conflict with one another. But these two elements together make up the Circumstances Orientation Motive.

Almost everyone has been in the situation where they have lost a client; perhaps a big one. This is an example of the Circumstances Orientation Motive in action. The first thing the boss does is look around for someone to blame (convenience). Usually some one person or group has to be the scapegoat, and it is just more convenient to put the blame on someone who is close by. Then, when that person or group has been identified and singled out, the pace picks up. Fire fighting is an example of how *convenience* and *pace* work together instead of separately. It can occur either way.

FIRE FIGHTING

There are a lot of organizations that appear to be dedicated to fire fighting. That is, they really don't seem to have a business plan that guides and directs them each day. Instead it's like a giant ship without a rudder. It drifts from one crisis to another, and we affectionately refer to this as *fire fighting* and to the people who work there as *fire fighters*. Businesses like this may have a business plan, but it is as if it is hidden away someplace or perhaps buried in the rubble from all the fires that have been fought. When an organization is dedicated to fire fighting it is completely engrossed in the Circumstances Orientation Motive to the *complete exclusion* of all other motives. When leadership is seen in this kind of a scenario, it becomes quite clear why the organization never gets anywhere. There is no time for team-building (membership), charisma (witness significance), time management, goal-setting (expectation), adaptation or any of the other motives discussed in this book. This is precisely why organizations that spend all of their time fighting fires (circumstances) never move ahead. Handling the day-to-day circumstances is all they can do, hence they are very limited as to how far they can grow or expand.

THE ARCHITECT'S PLAN

This book provides a blueprint for going beyond the firehouse. All eleven motives have to be considered. The difference between a leader and someone who is not a leader is that the leader is intimate with eleven motives. The firefighter knows only two, three or four of these motives and therefore cannot ever see the big picture. Firefighters only work when a fire is raging out of control. Otherwise they have coffee, play checkers or basketball and talk with their friends. Firefighters are loaded for bear when a fire is raging out of control, but when there is no fire, they are asleep at the switch. At the center of the firehouse is the firefighter's pole, which he or she slides down when the alarm goes off. Otherwise, the firefighter sleeps in the bunkhouse. Also, when there is no fire raging out of control, firefighters spend their time washing and polishing the equipment, so that when taxpayers ride by the firehouse they see the pretty, bright and shiny fire engines. But that's all they see: the veneer and the surface. They don't see what's underneath.

The pyramid of human motivation presents the whole picture in the form of the eleven motives discussed in this book. When we look at an efficient organization we not only see people all moving in the same direction but the trained eye can see what's moving them: time orientation, place orientation, expectation (goals), and adaptation (teamwork). And most of all, orientation to person (self) and spiritual survival (charisma and membership). That's what leadership is all about. Leadership *is* motivation.

LET THE CREATIVE JUICES FLOW

Most people, when asked, would say they are not very creative. They just don't have that creative spark. To disprove that assertion, we often ask them to get up early in the morning. By early, we mean 3:30 or 4:00 A.M. There are very few who will comply with this request, but the few who do notice a discernible difference. It's not that people aren't creative; it's just that they don't want to get up that early.

Why is it that you are more likely to be creative—at whatever your chosen field of creativity might be—at 4:00 in the morning? Most people, when asked, will say that "It's because the kids are still asleep" or "It's quiet and peaceful at that time of the day." And they are correct. Circumstances! At this time of the day there are no circumstances. The right side of the brain has not had the opportunity to be clouded, choked and cluttered with circumstances. It is free to make connections with other interests and projects on the left side of the brain, with motives on the right side and with emotions in the limbic system of the midbrain. Put another way, connections are easier to establish because of the absence of circumstances. This makes early morning an ideal time to bring closure or resolution to projects and enterprises, business or personal, and to come up with new strategies, diagnoses, implementations and other game plans that may have never occurred to you while you were actually working on a project. Most of the people we have suggested this to have found that it works!

It's interesting to note how we came up with this "discovery" in the first place:

Radio stations sell morning "drive time" for a premium. The reason: During the hours of morning drive time, thousands of people are held captive in their automobiles as they sit in traffic jams and snafus that pile up in many parts of the city, and particularly on the interstate system. But the problem is that drive time is expensive, and if a station includes too much advertising its listeners will change their loyalty to another station. Our strategy was to get them to change some of their advertising to "pre-drive time." The reason is that people are just waking up and they are in that magical and mystical state that occurs between fast asleep and wide awake. Their minds are uncluttered. They are wide open to suggestion. And to repeat what we said earlier, circumstances—whatever they may be—have not yet started their all-out attack on the mind. Those stations that took the plunge and made this switch were glad they did. They were happy because their clients were happy. Messages that emanate from a clock radio signaling you to wake up at 5:30 A.M. are much more effective than messages that come at the end of a 7:00 A.M. traffic report while you are sitting in your car, watching the clock and knowing that you are going to be late for work. The reason? No chaos. No circumstances. No clutter.

DISCONNECTING: "YOU DESERVE A BREAK TODAY!"

When you disorient from circumstances you disconnect. You get away from the things that come at you every day and threaten to drive you under. You disconnect from the *pace* with which you are familiar. You may go to the cabin at the lake or you may go to the library. Generally, although not always, disorientation from circumstances involves going someplace or being somewhere that is different from the daily routine.

As in all of the motives we discussed here, disorientation can be dangerous. It can be overdone. Or it can be done at the wrong time (Time Orientation Motive) or wrong place (Place Orientation Motive).

The example given in chapter 12 of the hospital recovery room employees having a Christmas Eve party while one of their patients was in critical condition shows how disorientation in any one of these motives can create multiple problems down the line. When the effective leader solves problems, he or she does not create further problems down the line. Some people refer to this trait as *vision*.

Conversely, no one can stay oriented to circumstances all the time. The advertising agency for McDonald's recognized this when it came out with one of the best remembered campaigns produced for this fast food giant: "You deserve a break today!" Like all advertising campaigns that work, it addressed directly one of the eleven motives in the pyramid of human motivation.

ONE MORE TIME: "YOU DESERVE A BREAK TODAY!"

A long-time business acquaintance and personal friend is happier today than he was the first twenty-five years of his career. He golfs almost every Wednesday afternoon. Until five years ago he drove himself hard every day, seven days a week. He was rewarded for his dedication to the job. He rose to a senior management position and was considered a "shining star" in his company. But about eight years ago something happened. His work pressures were showing, his wife of eighteen years was talking divorce and one of his three children was having serious discipline problems at school. He said all of this caught him by surprise.

The reason that it caught him by surprise was that he focused on nothing but work. Because of this, everything suffered. He had no outlet. His orientation was his job. He had no hobbies, and when he did spend time at home, he was preoccupied with thinking about work. He liked having this preoccupation. He loved his job; he liked what he did; he respected his staff; and he thought of nothing else.

Almost by accident he stumbled into golf. At first he was frustrated. But then he got hooked. Soon the pleasure of spending time on the golf course every other Wednesday gave way to a conclusion. What he eventually realized was that this new orientation allowed him to reorient to other circumstances in his day-to-day life. He began thinking clearer. He relinquished more responsibility to his subordinates. At home he focused on the family. He and his wife were once again able to talk. Together they began dealing with their child's problems at school. Every aspect of his life took on a new pace. A sense of renewal and stability allowed him to operate with a new perspective.

Quite simply, he allowed himself to alter his orientation to circumstances by establishing golf as a relief mechanism. It worked!

He doesn't get to golf every Wednesday, but he does get out on a fairly regular basis in order to renew and forget the everyday hassles. Because of this he is dealing with the day-to-day issues on all fronts in a healthier, happier and more productive manner. On top of this his handicap is eight!

WHAT'S YOUR TITLE?

We recently consulted for a large organization with fifty-two divisions or profit centers. Our assignment was to help complete some already planned organizational changes. However, it soon became apparent that we were up against a very unexpected phenomenon.

Each of the locations had a general manager, who in turn reported to one of six regional vice presidents. The regional vice presidents reported to the senior vice president of operations. The senior vice president reported to the company president. Our assignment was at the location, at profit-center level. As we began, we discovered the organizational changes already planned would not be as quickly introduced as all had assumed.

The first general manager to whom we were assigned almost immediately confided in us that he knew the changes were coming, but went on to say they would not fix what was wrong. He stated that there was no time to perform his job, or any management job. He did not see how making changes and reorganizing along product lines would help without adding more personnel. As that was the extent of our assignment, we at first met his observations with polite silence, but with no opinion.

However, his comments intrigued us. This was a large, successful and growing company. This particular general manager also seemed intent on assuring us that most of his peers believed that additional personnel were needed in order to meet day-to-day demands. There simply was not enough time in the day to do all that had to be done.

In spending a little time observing the day-to-day activities of this general manager, we quickly discovered what the problem was. He was not a general manager. He was at best a department manager, but actually performed the duties of a project coordinator! Everything went over his head and he didn't even realize he was not functioning like a general manager.

In the course of a week, he had fifteen to twenty calls, or an average of four per day from his boss (the regional vice president). These calls focused on minutiae and details that belonged at least two levels down. He was questioned by his boss about: (a) equipment speed on one of his six production lines for the previous day (this was asked eight different times during the week), (b) personnel questions concerning a particular supervisor who had once worked with the regional vice president in another location, (c) four specific accounting questions that required immediate responses (including investigation), and (d) five questions regarding sales issues. There were also several other detailed questions.

All of the questions required follow-up, investigation and the general manager's time. In all cases, the questions were about details that were the broad responsibility of the location's general manager, but should not have required the vice president's time nor the general manager's time. They were overwhelmed with details, or circumstances. It was micro-management. Not only was it time-consuming (time orientation), but it distracted all involved from performing their real jobs. This organization did not need additional personnel, it needed to manage the roles at the level they worked. For purposes of our illustration, this general manager and his subordinates were motivated by the Circumstances Orientation Motive to assume this micro-management approach to their jobs. It applied throughout the organization. It took everyone's time. The element of pace was obvious. Also their behavior included the Time Orientation Motive because time was being wasted. Department managers were behaving like supervisors, and no one had any time left over for strategic thinking.

The repair of this situation was difficult, but obtainable. It required both a vertical and lateral fix. A *vertical fix* is required when the blocks in the pyramid get out of order. As they did in this case. The Circumstances Orientation Motive had to be put back into the pyramid where it belongs: on the bottom. Not that circumstances are not important. It is just that they can be performed by individuals at a lower level in the organization.

A *lateral fix* is required when a person—in this case, the general manager—has gone out too far on one of the blocks in the pyramid. He had become too absorbed in details and minutiae. He had become so absorbed that he was overwhelmed!

The vertical fix moved the Circumstances Orientation Motive back to its rightful place in the pyramid. The lateral fix moved the manager further toward a "center stage" position on the Circumstances Orientation Motive.

REFERENCE

Fleischman, P. (1990). *The healing spirit.* New York: Paragon House.

Chapter 15

The Adaptation Motive and Leadership

TO BE OR NOT TO BE, OR TO BE LIKE EVERYONE ELSE

Because much of our work has been in advertising and consumer behavior, we inevitably had to deal with the Adaptation Motive, or the motive to be like everyone else and to do what they do.

The Adaptation Motive is, like all the motives discussed in this book, necessary for survival. Therefore, it is found in all of the animals on the planet, regardless of how advanced or primitive. MacLean (1990) indicated that as soon as infant reptiles are born they scurry into the deep cover of the forest in order to avoid being cannibalized by their own parents who would eat them for dinner. Lorenz (1935), in his extensive work with ducks, found that there were "critical periods" in which newly hatched baby ducks would attach themselves to and follow anything that moved. That critical period was within the first twenty-four hours after hatching. This landmark study was generalized to many other species and particularly to human infants, who within a certain time frame will "bond" to their caretaker, and apparently the caretaker to them. This bonding lasts a lifetime, and when it does not occur, for reasons of illness or neglect or for any other reason, the result is disturbed and disordered behavior that may last a lifetime. Basically, we need other people.

In a study of nonverbal behavior (Maddock and Fulton, 1994), we found that adaptation, in the form of moving the hands to the face, is a way of adapting to the inuterine environment for the human infant. That behavior continues after birth, which is why the mother has to keep the infant's nails neatly trimmed for the first six months so that the face will not be scratched and clawed.

ADAPTATION AND DEVELOPMENT: THE URGE TO BE LIKE EVERYONE ELSE

As life begins and up until the beginning of school, the child's primary exposure is to his or her parents. Entering school brings the child into a new world, in which there are many other people present who impact on the child's development. He or she begins to *imitate* those people and what they do. Imitation is the primary learning process in the early years. The child watches and then imitates what he or she sees. That's how everything gets started in the beginning.

In adolescence, we see girls walking down the street, all dressed in the exact same outfit, almost to the imprint on the bottom of the tennis shoes. And yet women, when they leave adolescence, have a desire to be unique and certainly not to wear the same dress as someone else. This does occur, nevertheless. Despite women's desire to be unique, they never want to be too unique. They basically still want to be like everyone else.

One of the unusual occurrences that pops up in adolescence is a phenomenon that is hard to explain. It is during adolescence that children make the decision of whether they should start to smoke. We know now, from our own research and the research of others, that they begin to smoke because their friends are smoking. It is strictly an adaptation phenomenon. So although they may choose to smoke for the right reason (everyone else is doing it), they nevertheless make the wrong decision. Smoking is injurious to one's health. However, this whole decision, which is almost always part of adolescence, brings into question the priority and strength of the Physical Survival Motive. Why would people want to do something to themselves that counters their physical survival needs? This is why physical survival in particular and motives in general are so hard to understand and again, why Maslow (1970) was wrong. If physical survival is so prominent and basic, why would people act on motives that were less prominent and less basic? We don't know all the answers, but we do know that it happens.

As adults, we adapt to what others do in almost everything that we do. The foods we eat, the clothing we wear and the homes in which we live. If we need to see a doctor, we ask our friends and neighbors for a recommendation. Similarly, if we need to see a dentist or want to know a good place to eat, we ask our friends who they see or where they go.

But it goes even further. As we all know, the fashion industry is built on the Adaptation Motive and what other people do. We see it in the form of testimonials. Someone that we respect says that he or she drives a Buick, and so we drive a Buick. Testimonials are one of the strongest forms of advertising and marketing because of the strength of the Adaptation Motive.

WATCH OUT FOR FLYING OBJECTS!

No where is the Adaptation Motive more clear than in corporate America.

We referred in chapter 10 to a large organization with which we consulted. While meeting in the corporate office over several days for planning purposes, we were able to observe a peculiar and unusual trait in many of the senior management and corporate staff with whom we met.

In meeting after meeting, and most noticeably when we were introduced to a new person, it seemed that simultaneous to the handshake and greeting, the person's head would tilt back ever so slightly, as if he or she were needing to peer at the handshaker through bifocal or trifocal lenses. This was true even if the person was not wearing glasses. Along with this gesture, the chin would be jutted out, the jaw lines squared up and in some cases they would squint their eyes just a little, as if they were having some difficulty with their vision. As mentioned previously, this occurred with roughly half the people that we met at corporate headquarters.

The literature of body language tells us that this can be a gesture of superiority in certain cases, particularly when the individual who does it is on his or her own home turf. What was puzzling, however, was that the gesture was so consistent from person to person, and had no bearing on the person's position within the company hierarchy.

By the fourth day it became more clear. Our contact there, a vice president, was walking us back to a small conference room when the company's CEO happened by. The vice president made the appropriate introductions, and as handshakes and greetings were exchanged it was clear that the CEO was peering at us through nonexistent bifocal lenses!

The corporate employees of this company may or may not have feelings of superiority, but what was occurring here was a clear demonstration of the Adaptation Motive at work. The motive to adapt to a behavior trait that was exhibited first by the CEO was strong. As a motive, adaptation is as strong as its elements, and the elements are status, belonging and acceptance by one's peers. We concluded that those wearing the "virtually invisible bifocals" were motivated by the need for security and self-confidence. They adapted in order to establish the fact that they were part of the team.

BROWN IS NOT A PRIMARY COLOR

Almost everyone in the corporate and business world knows that it is imperative to "dress for success." Dressing for success is a universally understood application of the Adaptation Motive. As youngsters, we wore only the sneakers that were in, the jeans that were worn by everyone else and did as others did. As adults, we continue to do this to establish our membership; that is to which group of people we belong. Interestingly, the dress code has a fairly rigid set of rules. For men, it means a dark suit, preferably blue or gray and a tie of the appropriate width. Because ties change in width by fractions each year, last year's tie will never work. A white, pastel or striped shirt is part of the uniform of the day. In fact, anyone wearing a short-sleeved dress shirt is immediately written off as a lightweight or a pretender. It's easy to remember back when as children we all wore the same jeans, tennis shoes and logo tee-shirts. Perhaps this was intended to prepare us for the business world and for the "dress for success" years.

Women have a little more freedom than men, but on closer examination they are also restricted. Only certain patterns are acceptable. A woman can wear a suit, or a shirt and a jacket. She can wear stripes or pastels, but these too have certain restrictions. There are rules about hem length, short-sleeved blouses and strict guidelines about showing cleavage. The basic rule for female attire is to neutralize one's gender while at the same time wearing female, not male clothing. As a footnote, these rules are a bit more complicated.

There are other intricacies and complications that are not as well known, but are nonetheless expected. For example, men are slowly beginning to wear brown suits again, but never in Philadelphia!

For blue-collar workers, a dress code requirement is also in place. In the absence of uniforms, most production workers understand that blue jeans and tee shirts, or a sweatshirt in the winter, are required and expected attire. But it doesn't stop there. Carrying one's lunch requires a one-person cooler with built-in carrying handle, only those failing to adapt would dare to carry a brown paper sack, or even the classic metal lunch pail with the "Thermos" bottle in the lid!

MONKEY SEE MONKEY DO

A subtle form of the Adaptation Motive exists in all organizations and actually helps to form or reinforce the organizational culture. For example, if the perceived norm of the reference group is to have affairs, then some will adapt to that behavior and will be likely to drift into a romantic affair. Likewise, if the norm is not to have romantic affairs, then that behavior will be adapted. Organizations that tend to allow and exhibit a lot of swearing and foul language will encourage that behavior, and if there is very little cursing then individuals will adapt to that norm. These norms are silent and hidden, and if practiced they can create a lot of anxiety and discord, but not a loss of money or a loss of one's job. They require an active choice on the part of the individual.

REFERENCES

Lorenz, K. (1935). Der Kumpen in der Uwelt des Vogels. *Journal of Ornithology 83*.

MacLean, P. D. (1990). *The triune brain in evolution: Role in paleocerebral functions*. New York: Plenum Press.

Maddock, R., & Fulton, R. L. (1994). *The silent side of communication*. Des Moines, IA: American Media. (book and video)

Maslow, A. H. (1970). *Motivation and personality*. New York: Harper & Row.

Chapter 16

The Expectation Motive and Leadership

LOOKING INTO THE FUTURE

The Expectation Motive is the feeling within everyone that causes them to trust, hope and hold to certain convictions about what the future has in store for them. Like the Adaptation Motive, the Expectation Motive is present almost from the beginning of life and it is not learned or taught by anyone. However, infants learn very quickly that there will be someone there to meet their needs and they come to expect that person—the caretaker—to be there when he or she is needed.

In the last thirty to fifty years, and at least since the great depression, Americans have come to look more and more to their government to fulfill the Expectation Motive. Although there is nothing wrong with this, the question is always asked "What happens when the well runs dry?" No one wants to face that possibility, and because of the strength of the Expectation Motive, it won't allow us to even consider that possibility.

The Expectation Motive is one of the five motivational groups that have been discussed, and it deals with the future, not the present. It assists people in adapting to the future and what is to come. The factor analysis we conducted on the basic motives revealed that the Expectation Motive consisted of two outlooks for people: those who look forward to the future with an optimistic outlook and those who look forward to it with a pessimistic outlook.

THE CINDERELLA SYNDROME AND THE 90/10/10/90
REVERSAL THEORY

An example of the Expectation Motive is seen in the *Cinderella Syndrome*, which has been described in the literature as it relates to women. It is a fact that more children in all corners of the world have been exposed to this fairy tale more than any other, and from what can be determined it dates back as far as the fifteenth century (Taylor, 1994). At issue is the belief that a young, handsome and sensitive man will come into a woman's life and rescue her from boredom and unhappiness. Danielle Steel, a very popular writer of books read primarily by women, has expanded on this age-old theme by wrapping it in a somewhat different disguise. Steel apparently recognizes that the one thing that women feel is missing in their lives when it comes to men is *sensitivity*. Ask most women what they would like to see more of in men and they will tell you they would prefer that men be more sensitive and understanding. All of Steel's books contain this paradigm, or theme: a sensitive man coming into the picture and acting as the rescuer, rescuing the heroine from insensitivity. This theme has an inherent appeal because it is directed at a motive that is already there: the Expectation Motive, or the belief that someone will come to the rescue. In this way, the Expectation Motive can leave women with an unrealistic view of the future.

In an unpublished paper (Maddock & Fulton, 1995), we observed the male counterpart to the Cinderella Syndrome in many factory workers with whom we have managed or with whom we have come into contact. In what we call the 90/10/10/90 Reversal Theory, we have found that as many as ninety out of one hundred workers have poor work habits because they believe, nonconsciously, that they will either inherit a large amount of money and will not need to work, or will be discovered, or win the lottery or win big at a casino. As a result, they believe that the "day job" is only to keep them occupied during this "holding period" until Ed McMahon knocks at their door with a fist full of cash. For that reason, they don't believe they will have to put forth that much effort working in mundane, repetitious and low-paying jobs until one of these events occurs. They are quite certain that an event like these will occur; the only question they have is when. It is our conclusion, however, that at best only ten out of the one hundred who await these magical events will ever strike it rich or be discovered. The other ninety will have to work in order to earn a living. So it works out to 10/100, rather than 90/100. Hence, the 90/10/10/90 Reversal Theory.

The Expectation Motive is integral in such diverse activities as choosing a physician or an attorney or going to a casino with the expectation of winning large amounts of money. Expectation is involved in risk-taking and in commissioned sales. Expectation is a strong, powerful force that assists individuals in dealing with the future. Of all the motives discussed in this approach to human motivation, the Expectation Motive is the one that has been the most heavily researched in psychology laboratories (see chapter 5).

THE EXPECTATION MOTIVE IN ORGANIZATIONS AND IN THE WORKPLACE

A senior executive was managing the human resources function of a large, 2,500-employee manufacturing firm. It became apparent that he was unable to take direct action. Although the organization considered itself as being on the cutting edge of employee empowerment, involvement and team-building, it was difficult for outsiders to see because of the limitations of the senior executive in charge. He did not appear to be involved in the process that initiated and oversaw these various aggressive personnel programs. Instead, he appeared detached and somewhat isolated from the personnel function.

This manager conducted weekly staff meetings in which the eight people reporting to him dutifully detailed the various activities, problems, solutions and hot-spots taking place in the facility. But he was rarely involved in these meetings and as just mentioned, appeared separated and disconnected from the activities going on around him, including this weekly staff meeting that he chaired. As a result, the staff was disjointed and lacked cohesion. There were obvious divisions within the staff. An increasing number of senior staff members became cynical, jealous and petty in their interactions with each other and with their subordinates. The newer staff members were earnest and enthusiastic and eager to make a difference, but this enthusiasm was always held in check by the more senior staff members.

This situation continued for two years, after which the plant became unionized. Employees said their decision to become a unionized plant was due to the uncaring attitude of management as well as what they called unacceptable working conditions, which included low wages, unsatisfactory policies, and so on. Employees felt the core management staff, which was typified by the nine-person human resources staff, was disengaged, disconnected and not in tune with the day-to-day operations of the plant. What was learned soon after the union came into the plant was that this senior human resource executive was indeed detached. He was a serious, addicted gambler. He wagered on virtually all sporting events, had several bookies and attended off-track parimutuel simulcasts with friends and acquaintances.

This situation is often seen in compulsive and addicted gamblers. They call bookies and other gambling associates as many as ten or twelve times per day from their workplace. They relegate their day job to second, third or fourth place in their lives. They appear detached because their minds are never on their jobs but are on the various bets they have placed for the day. They become disoriented to time, place and circumstances, as their bodies are at work but their minds are at the race track. In the case of this individual, he had done quite well with his gambling activities, and he had even managed to amass a sizable "nest egg" for his retirement. In a way, this is an application of the 90/10/10/90 Reversal Theory in action. But not only had the senior executive's preoccupation led to the discouragement of the employees, but his disinterest and disorientation at work had turned the optimistic expectation of some of the junior staff members into pessimistic expectation and a sense of hopelessness. This is an example of the Expectation Motive out of control, and how it can work in a negative direction as well as a positive direction.

THE EXPECTATION MOTIVE CAN DELIVER PERFORMANCE ABOVE AND BEYOND EXPECTATIONS

A small, eighty-employee company that manufactured space-age and aircraft adhesives was struggling to survive under the leadership of an owner who was an alcoholic and who cared very little about the business. The production manager was, on the other hand, concerned and involved in the company but negative expectation led him to become more and more discouraged. Eventually, the plant was threatened with closure and the owner's wife, who had committed her husband to a hospital for treatment of addictions, was forced to sell the plant. The production manager, seeing an opportunity in the marketplace, gathered a small group of investors and was able to raise enough money to make a down payment on the plant and its inventory along with one year's operating capital. His first move was to ask the employees if they would like to be members of a winning "team." He explained that they planned to triple production in the first year, tap markets that were basically unserved and get away from government contracts that created more headaches than they produced revenue. Of the eighty employees, seventy signed on. The production manager began having weekly and at times daily meetings with all the employees. Plant conditions were upgraded. Jackets, caps and tee shirts were handed out in order to make employees feel they actually belonged to something. Productivity was back up to a break-even point within six months, and in the next two months fifteen more employees were put to work. New contracts were brought in mostly through the efforts of two of the investors working with the production manager. It was also discovered in the process of "renewal" that the old owner had cheated some of his customers by diluting some of the formulas. This problem was made good by the new owners. Within one year, the plant was functioning at full capacity, attempting to hire more employees and to expand the production and warehousing facilities.

There are several motives involved in this example. The production manager, after becoming a part owner and plant manager, went to the employees with an offer. The offer consisted of joining a winning team and coming to meetings whenever they are held. Joining a winning team is an example of membership, one of Fleischman's (1990) elements of spiritual survival. The fact that the plant manager met with the employees, almost daily, and offered optimistic, confident and encouraging predictions for the future—and in fact met those predictions—is another example of Fleischman's elements of spiritual survival: witness significance. The manager had a genuine concern with each employee, knew them all by name and spent more time with them in the production area than he did in his air-conditioned office.

From the employees' perspective, they were fired up to produce. The plant manager and the new situation continually directed their attention to the future and to the expectation that they were progressively moving toward a new and rewarding future. Turnover during that time slowed considerably. Expectation and the Expectation Motive on the part of the employees actually turned the whole situation around, with the plant manager acting as the coach and introducing spiritual survival into the situation. At the end of the year, a party was held off premises to celebrate their victory and to disclose plans for the next year. This is an example of how the Expectation Motive can work in a positive direction, which it usually does. Some companies (Eastman, Federal Express) have used this same approach—combining the Spiritual Survival Motive with the Expectation Motive—to move forward and win the Malcolm Baldridge award for excellence.

REFERENCES

Fleischman, P. (1990). *The healing spirit*. New York: Paragon House.

Maddock, R. C., & Fulton, R. L. (1995). *Has Santa Claus really sabotaged the work force?* Unpublished paper.

Taylor, S. (1994, spring). "Cinderella" and the phallic foot: The symbolic significance of the tale's "slipper" motif. *Southern Folklore 52*(1), 19–31.

Chapter 17

The Combination of Leaders and Motives Creates a Return to Action, Performance and Productivity (Beyond all Expectations)

TWO PROBLEMS ADDRESSED

As most everyone knows, there are emotional elements in business and industry just as there are at home and in any other context. This book has addressed constructive ways to harness emotion so that it will produce results and earn interest. Unlocking emotion is the key to effective leadership. Unlocking emotion is the key to instigating motivation, and motivation is the key to effective leadership. In fact, we have known that all along. We just haven't practiced it.

The case histories outlined in this book attempted to show how so many managers turn their backs on emotional issues in hopes they will go away. But they never do. As any psychotherapist will attest, the denial and repression of emotion is a direct route to a powder keg. Powder kegs don't always ignite unless they are exposed to a spark, but who wants to take that chance? In addition, when the emotional climate is ignored, the keys that unlock the motivational secrets of the mind are also overlooked or ignored.

The following example provides an excellent illustration of how emotion is not only denied and ignored, but is actually battered back and forth like a hot iron that no one wants to touch for fear of getting burned.

A thirty-eight-year-old married man had been with a midsized midwestern manufacturing facility for twelve years. During the first ten years, he was a customer service representative (CSR), often calling on customers in the field and doing routine trouble shooting.

Because of his experience with customers, it was felt by a regional plant manager and by the sales manager during a transition that he would do well in sales. But at the end of his first year in sales it was quite clear that he was not a salesman and would not succeed. He was unable to even get close to his established and agreed on quotas.

Because he reported directly to the sales manager, it was the sales manager's job to orchestrate the termination. The sales manager procrastinated, however, eventually transferring him to another sales division, rationalizing that he would probably do better in another division. But he didn't. There was no reason to suspect or believe that he would. Place orientation had nothing to do with his inability to sell. This is an example of dealing with the wrong motivation, for the wrong reasons.

His supervisor in the new division insisted that he be terminated because his numbers were consistently down each quarter. But rather than terminate him, he sent him back to his first sales manager who had already procrastinated and deferred making a decision in order to avoid a confrontation. After several weeks, the first sales manager called the plant manager and asked him if arrangements could be made to secure his old job back again as a CSR. The plant manager did not really want to do this, and hesitated in his decision. At the time that this book was being written, no firm decision had been made and the "salesman" was still in his sales job, turning in ever decreasing numbers each quarter and not reaching his quotas.

Terminating an individual, especially one who has been with a company for many years, is a very emotional issue. In this case, three individuals who were responsible for making such a decision avoided making it for more than two years. This case history demonstrates how far managers in business will go to avoid a potentially emotional issue. This is not leadership. The people involved were not leaders. However, their procrastination is understandable, and here's why.

There is no business school, no textbook and no seminar that gives managers and businessmen the handle on how to deal with emotional issues. There are no consultants who can come in and write out a blueprint on how to handle subordinate emotions and inspire motivation, which is the purpose of this book. Industrial psychologists, who are often brought in as consultants, don't deal with emotion. Typically, psychologists deal with learning, and learning is a left-brain phenomenon. Emotions originate in the limbic system of the brain (midbrain) but are mediated and adjudicated by the right side. Ashworth (1995), who has been referenced in several chapters in this book, deals effectively with the issues of emotion and motivation in organizations.

NOT ROCKET SCIENCE

As we have presented emotional issues in this book, they are obviously not the deep-seated, pathological and borderline kinds of emotions that involve psychosis, severe neurosis or insanity. These kinds of problems, when they occur, are conspicuous and flagrant and it is not expected that they be handled by even the most seasoned or experienced leaders. These are the kinds of problems that are handled by professional psychiatrists. But even before that step, when a person becomes dangerous to him- or herself or endangers the welfare and well-being of other employees in the organization, management usually takes very quick and decisive steps toward termination. There is no alternative when people are placed in danger. But this situation, which involves deep-seated and dangerous psychopathology, although it exists, is rare. It is not the purpose of this book to address it or try to manage this kind of emotion because it is outside of the purview of management.

Conversely, the emotions that are found in the pyramid of human motivation are found every day, day by day and hour by hour and are a part of every plant, school, hospital or workplace that exists. Knowing that it exists and that it underlies the entire organizational structure and fabric of the workplace makes it much easier to deal with these emotional issues as they arise. Furthermore, the motives have now been identified. Previously and without the pyramid, there was no emotional framework or paradigm within which leaders could work and see that they were getting results for their efforts.

The kinds of emotions and emotional problems presented here are really not problems; they are opportunities. We should look at them as such and call them opportunities rather than problems. As part of the solution, we have presented a simple, eleven-step structure that has empirical, neurological and real-world (advertising) validation, and also allows the leader to get a handle on emotion and emotional issues. We call it the *pyramid of human motivation*. This structure also allows leadership to deal directly with motivation, rather than indirectly and ineffectively, as in the example just presented.

THE WAY THINGS OUGHT TO BE

The pyramid of human motivation shows how things should be. But they are not always that way. Knowing that, the effective leader can put the blocks back in place again and then reap the rewards of a finely tuned organization that is running on all eight cylinders. Consider for just a moment the waste of time, energy and money that has gone into that one individual in the example about the CSR turned salesman. Consider how much more effectively it could have been handled if those in charge had a handle on the underlying emotional and motivational issues.

Repairing the situation consists of putting the blocks back into their correct positions so that the emotional turmoil is ended. We refer to this as the *vertical fix*, because when the blocks get out of order, they go either up or down. For example, the salesman who believes the only way he can close a sale is to take clients out on the golf course three or four times before closing, has moved the Play Motive six levels up, above the Territorial Survival Motive. Another way to look at this is that emotional priorities are always getting shifted around, and when they are put back in order (vertical fix), the emotions that are being used in nonproductive activities can then be used in productive ones.

Chapter 12 discussed a boy who almost died because the hospital staff had transposed the blocks in the pyramid. Instead of channeling their energy into saving lives (Physical Survival Motive, which is why hospitals exist), they were having a Christmas Eve party (Place Orientation Motive and Time Orientation Motive). As noted on the pyramid (Figure 3.1), these two Orientation Motives fall well below the Physical Survival Motive. Even though they were paid to work overtime on Christmas Eve, they felt that they were entitled to have a party and more importantly, the party took priority over saving lives.

Now let's take a detailed look at how the pyramid was built, how it comes undone and how it can be put back together. Because that is the real challenge of leadership.

THE *REAL* CHALLENGE OF LEADERSHIP

It has been written that:

Humpty Dumpty sat on a wall.
Humpty Dumpty had a great fall.
All the king's horses and all the king's men
Couldn't put Humpty Dumpty together again.

It took about twenty-five years to construct the pyramid of human motivation, which in this case is the great wall. But we really can't take credit for building it. It was there all along. We just didn't know about it. But enough said about the wall. Now let's look at the fall.

There are three kinds of falls, which we have already touched briefly on and now want to examine in depth.

The First Kind of Fall

The first kind of fall is the kind Humpty Dumpty took. This is the worst kind of fall because he couldn't be put back together again. The plant manager who was introduced in chapter 13 had to be terminated, not because he did not respect his supervisor's time but because he had a deep-seated personality or characterological problem that caused him not to respect anyone's time, including his own. It is doubtful if he would ever change or be any different. If it is or was possible for him to change, then that would be the job of a professional psychiatrist and not the job of a leader. No vertical or horizontal fix would correct this problem. When the fall is of the nature of the one that Humpty Dumpty had, it is beyond the capabilities of any corporate leader or manager and for the most part, beyond the capabilities of anyone.

The Second Kind of Fall and the Vertical Fix

The second kind of fall is not nearly as devastating as that taken by Humpty Dumpty. The second kind of fall can be easily repaired by an effective, efficient and proficient leader after he or she learns the practice and principles of the vertical fix. This kind of fall involves fixing the wall itself, and not Humpty Dumpty.

At times, the wall comes apart. The building blocks, for one reason or another, become transposed. Blocks that should be of lesser importance take on the perspective of being more important than they really are. Another way of saying this is that priorities get shifted around, and little things all of a sudden become big things. And big things—the ones that need to be attended to right away—get left undone or unmanaged.

Let's look at some examples: People begin to smoke for one reason and continue to smoke for quite a different reason. They begin to smoke because their friends are all doing it. This is particularly true if smoking begins between the ages of sixteen and twenty-two, which is usually the case. This is when almost all people start to smoke. This is an example of the Adaptation Motive.

People continue to smoke for quite a different reason: they are addicted. Even tobacco companies now admit that cigarette smoking is addictive. And so they continue to smoke because of the Physical Survival Motive.

But aren't cigarettes detrimental to physical survival? Of course they are. But then why would people continue to smoke in the interest of physical survival? The reason is that there are two sides to every motive. When it comes to the Physical Survival Motive, there is the healthy side (smoke-free) and the addictive side. We see this very clearly in another example that deals with the Physical Survival Motive: food. There is the healthy, "eat lean" side, and the other side that wants to eat everything in sight. A person cannot only transpose blocks in the pyramid, requiring a vertical fix, but can also go to one extreme or another within one motivation or block on the pyramid. When this occurs, we call this the *lateral fix*.

Another example: An alcoholic begins to drink because of the Circumstances Orientation Motive. He or she wants to "wash away" the circumstances of the day: a lost client, a kid in trouble at school, another pass over for the vice president's title, losing money in the commodities market. That's why the beginning alcoholic starts to drink.

Like the smoker, the alcoholic continues to drink because, in this case, of two entirely different motives: the Physical Survival Motive and the Personal Orientation Motive—the Physical Survival Motive because of addiction, and the Personal Orientation Motive because of disorientation from who he or she is. Because alcoholics don't like themselves very much, they want to disorient from themselves. No one has much self-respect if they lose all self-control.

As pointed out with smokers, there are two sides to every motive (lateral fix). In the case of alcoholism, as in smoking, there are two sides to the Physical Survival Motive: the addicted side and the healthy side. In the case of the Personal Orientation Motive, there is the side that has mastered self-control and the side that has lost all semblance of self-control.

A third example of "unraveling" or disentangling and applying the vertical fix is taken from a situation where the Expectation Motive and the Territorial Survival Motive are exchanged. In the pyramid of human motivation these motives are very close, but the Territorial Survival Motive takes priority over the Expectation Motive in some situations, particularly in business and in organizations. Like all of the motives in the pyramid and the ones previously described, these two motives have a positive and a negative side. We have referred to this as the lateral fix. For example, on one side of the Expectation Motive there is the extreme optimist, and on the other side is the extreme pessimist. Higgins (1997) referred to these two different outlooks as the *promotion focus* (which is closer to optimism) and the *prevention focus* (which is closer to pessimism). The promotion focus has a primary anticipation of accomplishment, and the prevention focus has a primary anticipation of safety or "playing it safe."

The Territorial Motive also has two sides. One side is cooperation, and the other side is competition. Obviously, one can become too competitive, in which case we are usually talking about greed. On the other hand, one can become too cooperative, in which case we are looking at a "sleeping with the enemy" scenario.

An advertising manager at Apex Advertising Agency was involved in a competitive struggle to uncover the key to winning a coveted account that would add another $5 million to the agency's gross billings. Several other agencies in the city were competing for the account, as well as several agencies from outside the city. The advertising manager had what Higgins called a promotion focus, but would be more accurately described as optimisim. Because he was an optimist, everyone enjoyed working for the manager and did their best to please him. As problems arose, he would take a very cheerful and auspicious approach, reassuring everyone that it would all work out and they should not worry. As the deadline for presentations approached, it became more clear that the list was being pared, for the prospects would not have time to listen to all of the different agency presentations. Competition became more heated and agency personnel began to hear rumors about who was going to present first, second, third, and so on. The account manager did not seem bothered by any of this and continued to maintain a reassuring and supportive demeanor. He assured other management and staff in the agency that Apex was not only a leader among agencies (in terms of gross billings) but that they had a fifty-year-old history and had the respect of everyone, not just in that city but in cities throughout the Midwest. When the deadline was down to three days before the presentation, the word came that Apex was out of the running and would not have the opportunity to make a presentation. Only three agencies were chosen, and Apex was not one of them.

The Third Kind of Fall and the Lateral Fix

The account manager in the previous example was a good candidate for the lateral fix. He had gone "way out on a limb" by moving out to the extreme outermost edge of the building block referred to as the Expectation Motive. He would also require a vertical fix, as previously suggested, because he had transposed the Expectation Motive and the Territorial Survival Motive on the pyramid of human motivation.

Major psychosurgery? Not hardly. The leader who is skilled and trained in motives and in their rightful structure in the hierarchy can, within several counseling sessions, help this advertising executive to become less optimistic and more territorial and competitive. In the process of doing this, the person who is doing the restructuring can help the counselee become more of a leader.

A lateral fix is required when a person moves too far out toward the outer reaches on any of the blocks in the pyramid (see Figure 17.1). To be even more specific, that manager can move too far out toward the end not only within a motivational block, but also within any one of the elements of that motivational block. For example, look at this case history of a manager who moved too far out on the spiritual survival block of the pyramid.

"Misty" was the warehouse manager of a large auto parts distribution firm located in the southeast. Her job was to make certain that the inventory was in place and she directly supervised a number of human parts-pickers as well as two mechanical parts-pickers. Misty was picked for the job because she was a very orderly, neat and organized person. In fact, the CEO said he had never met anyone who was quite so well organized, and that this was an extremely important trait in an employee who had to keep track of thousands of auto parts.

However, what the CEO did not know was that Misty was an obsessive-compulsive personality. This is a characterological disorder, the kind that is not very amenable to treatment or a "fix" (American Psychiatric Association, 1994). Misty did not show these traits as a subordinate, but as soon as she moved into a managerial position they began to surface. She started to detail her subordinates to cleaning out parts bins and applying a liquid cleaner to all the parts in the bin as well as to the bin itself. She increased the number of times that she would do this, from once or twice a year to monthly. She began shifting and consolidating parts and bins. The warehouse began to experience significant delays in parts delivery and the customers, who were all wholesalers, started to complain. Like the librarian who feels that his or her job is not complete until all of the books are safely back on the shelves, Misty seemed to have a strange attachment to the parts and hated to see them leave the warehouse after they had been so neatly cleaned and stacked in their bins. It was not long before customers began to cancel their orders and Misty had to be counseled about her priorities.

Figure 17.1
Vertical and Lateral Fixes

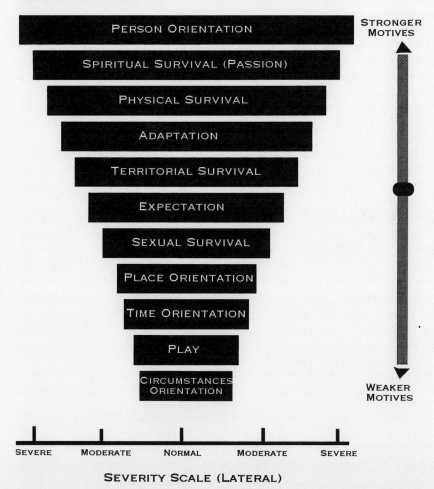

PERSON ORIENTATION

SPIRITUAL SURVIVAL (PASSION)

PHYSICAL SURVIVAL

ADAPTATION

TERRITORIAL SURVIVAL

EXPECTATION

SEXUAL SURVIVAL

PLACE ORIENTATION

TIME ORIENTATION

PLAY

CIRCUMSTANCES ORIENTATION

STRONGER MOTIVES

WEAKER MOTIVES

SEVERE   MODERATE   NORMAL   MODERATE   SEVERE

SEVERITY SCALE (LATERAL)

Remember, the motive involved here is spiritual survival. What's spiritual about auto parts? Auto parts within themselves are not a spiritual issue. The spiritual issue here is the element of *lawful order*. Misty, as an employee, did an excellent job of sorting, stacking and detailing parts. Furthermore, she did not allow anything to stack up in the warehouse or collect a lot of dirt, dust or grease. It was only after she became the manager that she imposed her own understanding of lawful order on the whole warehouse staff, which eventually began to affect customer relations and sales.

A *lateral fix* is required here. Misty, with counseling, was gently guided back to a more reasonable position by her supervisor, who understood the pyramid of human motivation. This was very difficult, because, as it was previously noted, Misty was characterological. She had an obsessive-compulsive disorder. Normally, this is difficult to treat, but new medications that are very effective in treating this disorder were also employed with the advice and assistance of Misty's family physician. Counseling and the lateral fix assisted in bringing her back to reality. In this case, the reality was that although parts cataloging and storage was a very important aspect of her job, customer relations and sales were even more important.

The situation involving Misty could have been interpreted as a Humpty Dumpty type fall, because she was characterological. However, in this case it was possible to salvage her. Without medication it would not have been possible because characterological disorders are generally very resistant to treatment and this is particularly true of obsessive-compulsive disorders. However, Misty's compulsivity was a highly desirable trait, and through lateral-fix counseling it was possible to maintain enough of that compulsion so that she could continue her effectiveness, but at the same time focus on the real mission of the parts house, which was to deliver car parts to customers in a courteous, efficient and rapid manner.

APPLICATIONS

The pyramid of human motivation goes beyond applications in the workplace. Obviously, it applies to recreational, social, business and nonbusiness relationships, but it is particularly applicable to the role of leaders and leadership. Nevertheless, this example relates to the application of the pyramid in the home.

A forty-eight-year-old accountant had been depressed and dysphoric. It got to the point where his clients began to avoid him because of his dysphoric moods. His wife suggested that he see a physician, which he did. The physician recommended 20 mg. of Prozac (fluoxetine) once a day. He purchased the medication and took it regularly.

It was not long before his wife began to complain that they were no longer having sex on a regular basis. Sexual encounters on the basis of two to three times a week had been reduced to once a month and eventually to once every two months. Her husband said he had noticed it but he was feeling so much better since he began taking the Prozac that it really didn't worry him. He said that things just seemed to be going a lot smoother and he was no longer looking for problems and complications in his life that weren't really there, which had been his problem in the past. His wife said he needed to discuss the situation with his physician. Once again he took her advice, but the doctor told him he was probably just tired and working too hard, and to take a vacation.[1]

A few days later, the man's wife read in the *Physician's Desk Reference* that Prozac and other antidepressants interfered with sexual functioning.

This illustration shows that the emotions we have described in the workplace also occur at home and in other settings. The accountant's wife said what she had learned in all of this was that despite the fact that her husband virtually ignored her sexually, her love for him never changed. She never doubted or questioned his love during this time, whereas in the past she had always felt that sex and love were inextricably bound up together and could not be separated from one another. In fact, she even referred to the sex act as "making love."

This is a case of confusing sex and love; a mistake made more often by women than by men. It is clearly stated in the pyramid of human motivation that sexual survival is an independent motive and consists of four elements: gender, inhibition, impulse and impotence. Nowhere in the pyramid does it state or imply that sex and love are related or connected. On the other hand, love is one of the elements of spiritual survival, and this is clearly demonstrated in research carried out by Fleischman (1990) and also in chapter 5 when we factor analyzed the elements Fleischman identified.

CONCLUSION

Why another book on leadership?

The answer by now should be crystal clear. There are probably more books and articles written on leadership than on any other subject in business. However, there is virtually no literature on the subject of motivation. When asked what motivates an employee, a customer, a client or a patient, we are strictly on our own. Our personal experience, after subscribing to an article update service for more than one year, is that few if any articles on motivation were ever delivered. The ones that were delivered were not on motivation at all, but involved studies of animal learning. A few involved studies carried out in education because educators (particularly at the elementary level) are very interested in motivation.

Leadership is motivation. Leaders are motivators. Orientation. Survival. Expectation. Play. Adaptation. Those are the motives. They are given to us at birth, or shortly afterward (and in some cases before) in a neat little package, which we have shown graphically as a pyramid. But along the way they get misplaced, lost, displaced or forgotten. Someone has to put the pieces back together. The good news is that leaders can do it, and if they don't know how, they can be trained. It borders on the absurd to say that leaders are motivators, but then not to define or specify the motives with which they are supposed to be working.

The good news is that the missing part of the puzzle—motives and motivations—have been found.

The bad news is that we can't put Humpty Dumpty back together again. But then most of us already knew that anyway. However, we can take the tools of motivation and get back in business. We can, in many cases, take the motives and motivations that threatened to destroy us and build on them, using them as resources in the same way that Eastman, Federal Express and other companies did, by applying the business of leadership.

Leaders are motivators, and leadership is motivation.

NOTE

1. Physicians are notorious for not telling their patients that all antidepressants cause sexual inhibition, in varying degrees. This is probably because they know that if they do reveal this information, patients will become noncompliant to the medication. Conversely, pharmacists will willingly and readily give out this information when asked.

REFERENCES

American Psychiatric Association. (1994). *Diagnostic and statistical manual of mental disorders* (4th ed.). Washington, D.C.

Ashworth, B. E. (1995). Emotion in the workplace: A reappraisal. *Human Relations 48*(2), 97.

Fleischman, P. (1990). *The healing spirit.* New York: Paragon House.

Higgins, E. T. (1997). Beyond pleasure and pain. *American Psychologist 52*(12), 1280–1300.

Suggested Readings

ARTICLES

Ashworth, B. E. (1995). Emotion in the workplace: A reappraisal. *Human Relations 48*(2), 97–127.

Cooper, R. (1997). Applying emotional intelligence in the workplace. *Training and Development 51*(12), 31.

Oncken, W. and Wass, D. (1974). Management time: Who's got the monkey? *Harvard Business Review*, November–December.

BOOKS

Bass, B. M. (1985). *Leadership and performance beyond expectations.* London: Collier-Macmillan.

Bass, B. M. and Stogdill, R. M. (1990). *Handbook of leadership: Theory, research and managerial applications.* New York: Free Press.

Drucker, P. F. (1973). *Management, tasks, responsibilities and practices.* New York: Harper and Row.

Farrell, W. (1986). *Why men are the way they are.* New York: McGraw-Hill.

Fleishman, P. (1997). *Cultivating inner peace.* New York: Tarcher-Putnam.

———. (1990). *The healing spirit.* Cleveland, SC: Bonne Chance Press.

Herzberg, F. (1959). *The motivation to work.* New York: John Wiley and Sons.

Klauss, R. and Bass, B. M. (1982). *Interpersonal communication in organizations.* New York: Academic Press.

Kohles, M. K., Baker, W. G. and Donano, B. A. (1995). *Transformational leadership: Renewing fundamental values and achieving new relationships in health care.* Chicago, IL: American Hospital Association.

Taylor, F. (1911). *Principles of scientific management.* New York: Harper and Row.

Vecchio, R. P. (1997). *Leadership: Understanding the dynamics of power in organizations.* Notre Dame, IN: University of Notre Dame Press.

Vroom, V. (1964). *Work and motivation.* New York: John Wiley and Sons.

Name Index

Subject Index

About the Authors

RICHARD C. MADDOCK is in the private practice of psychology and is licensed in Arkansas and in Tennessee. He is board certified in psychology, holding the ABEPP certification. He is also a member of the Arkansas Psychological Association and the American Psychological Association. He is an Assistant Professor at Arkansas State University in Jonesboro, where he teaches statistics and research design. Dr. Maddock regularly conducts research and seminars on motivation and leadership for businesses and other groups.

RICHARD L. FULTON is Vice President of a $7 billion magazine and book printing company with worldwide locations. He has also served as a division president of another large commercial printing corporation, and as a private business consultant. Published in various trade publications, he has co-authored *Marketing to the Mind* (Quorum Books, 1996) with Dr. Richard Maddock, as well as several video-based training modules. He is frequently called upon to speak about leadership, organizational change and motivation.